THE POWER OF SEVEN-SECOND CHANCES:

Obtaining Success Without Firing the "Rest"

Nicole D. Price | Dr. Ian Roberts

The Power of Seven Second Chances
Obtaining Team and Organizational Success Without Firing the Rest

Nicole D. Price and Dr. Ian A. Roberts

Copyright Pending
The United States Copyright Office

No parts of the publication may be reproduced, distributed or transmitted in any form or by any means, including photocopying, recording, or other electronic or mechanical methods, without the prior written permission, except in the case of brief quotations embodied in critical review and certain other noncommercial uses permitted by copyright law. Submit permission requests, at www.livelyparadox.com

Cover imagery: Ashley Gaffney Designs
The Power of Seven Second Chances by Nicole D. Price and Dr. Ian Roberts
1st ed.

ISBN-13: 978-1543004281

ISBN-10: 1543004288

This book is for every person who understands that there are reasons and causes uniquely worthy of our own personal leadership development - the people at the end of all those data points.

TABLE OF CONTENTS

INTRODUCTION
Why This Topic?
Empathy and Compassion Unpacked

PART ONE
Chapter One – The Traditional Way
Chapter Two – The Trickle-Down Effect
Chapter Three – Leading Empathetically and Compassionately

PART TWO
Chapter Four – Interrupting the Cycle Using Seven Second Chances
Chapter Five – Seven Quick Guidance Points
Chapter Six – The Price-Roberts Model
Chapter Seven – The Conclusion: Optimum Conditions for Success

ABOUT THE AUTHORS

ADDITIONAL RESOURCES

The Power of Seven Second Chances

Why This Topic?

In management circles, few names elicit as powerful a mix of admiration and contempt as the name Jack Welch. Love him or hate him, the longtime chairman and CEO of General Electric is one of the most influential figures in modern management. Shortly before his retirement in 2001, *Fortune* magazine named him "Manager of the Century" in recognition of his outstanding record – under his leadership, GE stock went up 4,000 percent. As for the less acclaimed aspects of his legacy, Welch is also known as a ruthless believer in productivity. As a manager, he subscribed to the idea of "hiring the best and firing the rest."

Welch was undeniably successful, so arguing with his approach requires a clear paradigm shift, and that's exactly what our project is about. We're proposing a whole new understanding of management, an approach diametrically opposed to the idea of "firing the rest."

Our first argument against "firing the rest" is philosophical and, perhaps, idealistic. A relentless and unforgiving focus

The Power of Seven Second Chances

on productivity promotes a culture of fear – an environment in which employees are more likely to compete against each other than to collaborate with one another. We believe this kind of environment is not the most conducive to growth and development, and we also know most people simply don't enjoy working under such conditions. And our second argument is plain and practical. Most organizations just cannot afford to "hire the best and fire the rest."

Employers of choice may fire the bottom 10 percent of their managers every year, just like GE did under Welch. And they may also hire among the top 10 percent of each graduating class as they replenish their management pool. But unless you're an employer of choice, your hiring and firing options are likely much more limited. Often you must choose among candidates with varying levels of skill, talent, or passion; only rarely do you find a strong balance of all three attributes. And when it comes to firing, most companies would do well to reserve that most extreme of measures for the most extreme of circumstances. Luckily, most do.

The Power of Seven Second Chances

You may be wondering how an educator with a record of success in public school turnarounds and a chemical engineer with years of management and consulting experience suddenly find themselves advocating for a new approach to leadership.

One of us started out as an "at-risk youth," one of those kids who was always in trouble, and he ended up competing in the Olympic games –thanks to a principal who was willing to give him a second chance. And one of us, with nothing but tough leadership as examples, spent years as a tough manager leading the way she'd always been led, until graduate work in adult learning taught her that people need more than force, facts, or fear to change their behavior – they need relationship and multiple opportunities to get it right.

We have come together to collaborate on this project because our very different experiences have led us to a common belief. Our professional paths have converged at the realization that most managers, like most educators, must build success with what they have. And in order to build

The Power of Seven Second Chances

success with what they have, they must take the time to understand, nurture, and develop what they have. While precise evaluation and decisive action may be the tools of an effective manager under the Welch model – a manager who may "fire the rest" – empathy and compassion are the quintessential tools of managers and educators who need to make the most of the people they have. And in case you're wondering whether evaluation plays a role at all in empathetic leadership, the answer is: Absolutely, but mostly as an information-gathering mechanism to guide growth and development.

Working, like we do, in urban education or community health, empathy and compassion are simply a must. Not only does work in these fields require a high degree of emotional intelligence, but also these sectors in general draw from a talent pool in which passion is much more abundant than training. This kind of work attracts workers inspired by the mission and the vision of their organizations, workers who are typically highly empathetic themselves, and workers who are neither motivated nor helped by unyielding standards. Leading these kinds of organizations requires an empathetic approach – an approach that both recognizes employees as resources worth developing and empowers them to treat and lead others empathetically as well.

But we're here to make an even broader argument. For years, statistics about American workers have been telling a bleak story week after week. Consistently, close to 70 percent of employees report being disengaged at work. Put another way, more than two thirds of American workers will not give discretionary effort; they will do only the bare minimum. We believe our business culture has oversubscribed to the idea of productivity at all costs, and engagement has suffered as a result. But we also believe leading with empathy and compassion can help re-engage the many employees whose motivation has caved under outsized performance expectations or, worse, faltered in the face of management inattention. We know there's a better way, and we know it all starts with empathy and compassion. Our hope is that the chapters that follow will help you chart the rest of the course.

Compassion and Empathy Unpacked

Many people often conflate empathy and compassion. The truth is, these words have very different meanings, but there is a very strong relationship in the arena of leadership. Empathy should be viewed as a gateway to compassion. It's a willingness to understand how someone or a group feels, trying to "walk a mile in their shoes" and thinking about how you might feel in a similar situation. On the other hand, compassion builds on empathy. It is a consideration of the emotional state. It is acknowledging that it's their feeling and emotion, refusing to deny it, and with intentionality, acting to alleviate the pain. Many people in the daily pursuits will ask those whom they encounter, "How are you?" without waiting for or really caring much about the response. Authentic compassion is an act of genuinely caring about the feeling, emotional, and mental state of individuals. The next time that you ask someone, a stranger or someone with whom you are acquainted, "How are you?" take the time to await and acknowledge their true response. Should such a response be negative or a cry for help, what will you do then? Will you dish out a dose of compassion? Will you be too busy to pause your day? Do you really have an interest in their response to your question? What if their response is: "I am not doing well, my dog died last night?" Will you further engage in an expression of sympathy, empathy, or compassion? As you read along in our book, it is important that we unpack the aforementioned three terms.

Sympathy

Sympathy is essentially the expression of sorrow for another's hurt or pain. The emotional connection between the person expressing sympathy and the person receiving may be miles apart because the person expressing is not experiencing the hurt, pain, or tragedy. In leadership, particularly empathetic leadership, you will later read that we caution against being sympathetic and risking coming off as someone who expresses pity for others. Pity is an emotion that tends to dehumanize and belittle, both actions that are contradictory to the expected outcomes of empathetic approaches to leadership. Expressing pity or sympathy in leadership can appear condescending at times. Case in point, individuals who are impacted and protected by the Individual with Disabilities Education Act, PL 94-142

The Power of Seven Second Chances

(IDEA) or the Americans with Disabilities Act (ADA) will vehemently oppose and even despise being 'pitied' as pity erodes the rich reality of their human experience and does not empower or inspire them.

Empathy

Empathy is the willingness of individuals or groups to recognize the emotional state of others. Unlike sympathy, empathy goes beyond the expression and acknowledgement of someone's pain and suffering, and puts one in a place whereby you demonstrate the ability to understand for yourself some of the pain that the other person or group may be experiencing. It is an acknowledgement of our shared experience as humans and recognition that we all feel grief and loss and pain and fear. You do not need to have experienced exactly the same events as the person who is suffering but you do need to have the ability to really imagine how they must be feeling in their situation. Empathy is a vicarious experience – if your friend or colleague is feeling afraid, you too will recall an experience when you have felt fear in your body; if they are sad, you too can remember a time when you felt sorrow. Feeling empathy is allowing yourself to become tuned into another person's emotional experience.

Compassion

Compassion and compassionate leadership is the verb-alignment of empathetic leadership or the action approach. Compassion is the transfer of the feeling of empathy into action that mitigates or alleviates the pain, hurt, challenge, or suffering of the person or group on the receiving end. You found out that a colleague is under the weather and unable to facilitate a scheduled meeting across town. In addition to expressing empathy (understanding) for their state of health, you offer to use their prepared agenda and talking points to stand in and facilitate the meeting on their behalf. Essentially, compassion is the ability and willingness to stand alongside someone and to put their needs before your own. According to the Dalai Lama, living a compassionate life can be learned – it is not just something that some 'extra-good' people are born with. Some have even described compassion in leadership as love in action. Changing habits takes persistence and practice but it is achievable through the right methods. Many of the worlds' wisest people have stated that giving to others in life is the source of the greatest contentment and life satisfaction, so there are many personal benefits to be gained as well."

Throughout this work we encourage everyone, those in positions of leadership and those who are embracing this approach for their personal life to do so from an empathetic orientation. Some people espouse that the heart and head cannot work together in tandem. There is a misconception that individuals in positions of leadership must choose one of the two ways to lead; either from the heart (guided by emotional intelligence) or with the head (guided by intelligence quotient). Those who have invested in the empathetic leadership approach and have done so with scalable success understand the importance of tapping into the various forms of empathy. There is a plethora of research that echoes the benefit of understanding the different forms of empathy. The first is **"cognitive empathy,"** simply knowing how the other person feels and what they might be thinking. Sometimes called perspective-taking, this kind of empathy can help in, say, a negotiation or in motivating people. **Cognitive empathy** is the largely conscious drive to recognize accurately and understand another's emotional state. A study at the University of Birmingham found, for example, that managers who are good at perspective-taking were able to move workers to give their best efforts. But there can be a dark side to this sort of empathy – in fact, those who fall within the "Dark Triad" – narcissists, Machiavellians, and sociopaths (see Daniel Goldman's *Social Intelligence*) – can be talented in this regard, while having no sympathy whatever for their victims. It is the belief of some that a torturer needs this ability, if only to better calibrate his cruelty – and talented political operatives no doubt have this ability in abundance. The immigration travel ban that was instituted in January 2017 by the newly elected President of the United States Donald Trump is an example. We witnessed, that this was amplified enormously by what appeared to be a lack of understanding around the undue pain, suffering, and life-impacting results on many individuals, groups, and families who the ban may not have intended to negatively impact. This suffering was compounded by the fact that the president and other elected officials were attacking the legitimacy and credibility of federal judges, political pundits, or anyone else with whom they disagreed. The cognitive empathetic approach of leadership suggests that it would behoove those in positions of leadership to pivot away from being detached and political, and embrace every perspective and position before finalizing decisions during a time of crisis.

Although the term "crisis" may take on a different meaning within different organizations, we are suggesting that empathetic and compassionate leaders are best suited to ensure the most effective and right outcomes under these circumstances. Certainly, empathy qualifies as one critical measure of the right leader in a crisis, along with being composed and collected under pressure. But exactly what kind of empathy should we look for? When it comes to the right leader for a crisis, cognitive empathy alone seems insufficient.

Then there is **"emotional empathy"** – when you feel physically, along with the other person, as though their emotions were contagious. This emotional contagion, social neuroscience tells us, depends in large part on the mirror neuron system (see Chapter Three in *Social Intelligence*). Emotional empathy makes someone well-attuned to another person's inner emotional world, a plus in any of a wide range of callings, from teaching, retail sales, and medicine; and in many instances, for many who have a relational connection - any parent, partner, or lover. One downside of emotional empathy occurs when people lack the ability to manage their own distressing emotions. This can be seen in the psychological exhaustion that leads to burnout. The purposeful detachment cultivated by those in K-12 education, community healthcare, or any other organizations whereby the constituents often have incredible challenges, offers one way to inoculate against burnout. But the danger arises when detachment leads to indifference, rather than to well-calibrated caring.

PART ONE

CHAPTER ONE THE TRADITIONAL WAY

If you review the mission and core values of successful organizations, you'll see that people are deemed important to their work and outcomes. Zappos is a good example. Tony Hsieh, the company's CEO, constantly points out that people want to be part of something bigger than themselves – they want a higher purpose. He consistently states that happiness is critical both at work and in life, and that focusing on happiness can change the world in ways bigger than we could ever imagine.

Tony Hsieh explained his belief in the importance of happiness in a keynote address delivered at Stanford University titled "Happiness Matters: How to Create a Culture for Business to Thrive." But what you should know is that this isn't hyperbole. The Hsieh philosophy has worked at Zappos, and it is the reason behind the company's swift leap from $1.6 million to $1 billion in revenue. Zappos has succeeded because of its relentless focus on the happiness of its people. The company says it in its mission statement, and

The Traditional Way

its behaviors match. Unfortunately, Zappos is an anomaly. If you take a deeper dive, look beyond the words in the mission statements and peek into the actions and behavior within most organizations, you will start to see that the bottom line appears to be more important than the people, let alone their happiness.

How do we know this? One common set of practices demonstrates this lack of alignment between word and deed in most organizations: performance management. If people are not contributing to the bottom line, or if they appear to have performance problems, companies typically employ a standard approach. When faced with employees whose performance is found to be less than stellar, companies resort to evaluation, criticism, exclusion, and ultimately expulsion or termination. These practices play out in specific ways in many organizations, and they tend to generate sadness, unhappiness, or disengagement: the antithesis of happiness.

Leaders who utilize an empathetic approach can look beyond an instance of underperformance or even "failure" and be inspired by someone's potential to become a "winner" or organizational contributor. This approach towards failure-inspired empathy transcends any one type of organization or team.

Failure-Inspired Empathy

Dr. Roberts has a personal story that supports the conceptual framework of failure-inspired empathy. In 1995, he was the first person in his family to possibly attend and graduate from college. However, he did not have the financial means to afford books for college, let alone tuition. Because of his academic and athletic ability, he believed he could likely get an athletic scholarship. He was talented in soccer and basketball but his abilities on the track would prove to be the route to college attendance. It is a great reminder that sometimes we believe that our talents are in one area, but later learn that competencies, abilities and talents are transferrable and can be used in other capacities.

The Traditional Way

In his first official 800-meter race, Dr. Roberts finished 3rd. The gun went off and he ran using every strategy that he could remember from his interactions with his coach. The truth is, after the first 400 meters of the race, he forgot about every coaching conversation and strategy that was shared with him. He often recalls how he just wanted to finish. In the final 100 meters, he was placing 6th but with the cheers of the crowd moved up three places. His coach responded, "There are girls who run faster!"

He remembers laying in the center of the field after his race and deciding that he would never run that event again. As the summer track season progressed, so did his times in the 800-meter. His time improved from 2 minutes and 1 second to 1 minute and 55 seconds. His coach insisted that "this was his race" and he ended up running that event or something similar 100 more times during his collegiate and professional track and field career. Consequently, his coach told him that he was probably on track to run fast enough to receive a partial athletic scholarship to college. The coach told Dr. Roberts that he believed that he had the discipline to get even better. As a result, his coach personally drove him to visit four potential universities. He was rejected by all four in a 24-hour period. Today, Dr. Roberts has a litany of educational and professional accomplishments. He has also run the 800-meter race at the Olympic level. Why? First, he was held to strict levels of accountability. He worked hard. He studied the best in the field. He made adjustments. He was committed. Second, his high school coach was a visionary and believed in what he could not see. And most importantly, because at least one college coach was willing to further develop him rather than evaluate him.

Whenever the discussion of "failure-inspired empathy" is discussed, we remind leaders that this approach requires leaders to have the foresight to see beyond someone's current performance and recognize that there is the potential for the person to improve or get better. Essentially, someone's failure should not be fatal. A solid leader is one who has enough visionto see the salvageable qualities in a person who has failed in one or more areas, and empathizes enough to see potential for improved performance.

The Traditional Way

Leaders have to be visionaries - to see beyond the present performance of candidate or direct report. The leader who models extreme empathy and vision will risk giving another chance (even multiple chances) to individuals who may have been rejected or evaluated poorly by others. Once you take this stand as a leader, you may win some and you will likely make some errors in judgement. Regardless, err on the side of taking your chances and use empathetic lenses to recruit. After all, the next All-American, Olympic athlete, employee of the month, high performer, or leader of the year may be at the other end of your actions and decisions.

The Amazing Race - A Strategic Approach to Inspire Empathy & Compassion in Education

To encourage the capacity building of an empathetic and compassionate approach to teaching and leading is understanding the customers - the people served. In education, the customer is the children. As a school leader in Dr. Roberts used a tool he called "Amazing Race." He advised superintendents and principals to focus their professional development at the end of summer break on two things; realignment of the school or district's mission, vision, and key strategies and engaging the community. In order to understand the customer (the children), teachers, staff and leaders must spend time in the shoes of the customer. The Japanese call this Gemba Genbutsu or "actual place, actual thing." Using the professional development session to visit the community helps everyone who participates in the "Amazing Race for Community Engagement" to connect with students, families, and members of the school community. The activity allows the teachers, staff, administrators, and other stakeholders to get a first-hand experience by interacting in the environment where their students reside.

Given the fact that empathy by its very definition means that someone understands and shares the experience and emotions of another person, this strategy allows for an attempt at authentic and meaningful engagement of the community. Dr. Roberts recalls that he first started this activity in the 2007 school year in Baltimore City, and its impact was incredible and served as the impetus for the

The Traditional Way

paradigm shift in parental engagement (exceeding 90%) for every school that he subsequently led. The "Amazing Race for Community Engagement" strongly encourages every adult who serves students to visit the homes and community of those students throughout the school year. Regardless of the type of school, district, or community; wealthy, middle class, or impoverished, it would behoove educators to visit and spend quality time understanding and eventually anchoring their pedagogy, leadership, and interactions from a place of empathy (Culturally Responsive Pedagogy and Leadership). This understanding is beneficial for the customer and it connects all the members of the organization in a meaningful way. It results in partnerships, but more importantly, in genuine friendships. The Gallup organization deems friendships so important that a company's engagement scores are dependent on employee responses to the statement "I have a best friend at work." Work-friendship increase workplace happiness and this reverberates throughout an organization.

In most organizations, the performance evaluation process is pretty standard, and employee happiness is typically the least of the concerns. Later we will share key strategic steps to help you avoid the pitfalls of perpetual underperformance and other negative outcomes associated with evaluation, criticism, exclusion, and termination. However, we think it is important that you take a keen look at the way we generally approach performance management today.

Evaluation

In every organization, the evaluation system is intended to create or drive accountability. While personal accountability is a driver of happiness, in this phase of the performance management process most organizations are not focused on locus of control or personal accountability. Often they are focused on accountability, responsibility, or ownership of outcomes: think "bottom line." Unfortunately, evaluation often instills and creates a culture of fear rather than one of personal accountability or even ownership. This is especially evident with new employees. An associate new to a team is bound to make missteps; this is inherent to starting a new job. Yet the onboarding process has a keen focus on the evaluative component. While it is imperative that a new employee understand what success looks like, evaluation has

The Traditional Way

a negative impact on the human psyche. Evaluation as we know it is a structured or formal system that guides the employee-supervisor relationship. The formal process is measured by looking at the employee's strengths and areas of growth to determine "fit" or effectiveness. Although the aim of most evaluation systems is to identify performance gaps, in too many instances the response from supervisors or agents of the organization is not necessarily to fix or to implement structures to close those gaps. Instead the response is to intimidate, penalize, or separate the person being evaluated from the position or organization. Many employees surveyed believe that evaluation conducted this way has a negative impact on their psyche. Conversely, a study on 360-degree feedback conducted by Arizona State University found that improvement in a leader's employee-development behaviors will lead to positive changes in employee development, job satisfaction, and engagement, and it will also reduce employees' intent to leave the organization. In other words, failing to focus on development and choosing to focus on evaluation have a negative impact on associates and is not shown to improve outcomes. What if the employee-supervisor relationship were rather than transactional?

It should be noted that new employees are not alone in this evaluation trap. Low performers and tenured employees whose skills may have become irrelevant are also burdened with evaluation. Because of tenure, these kinds of employees receive the added pressure of additional evaluation tools such as the performance improvement plan (PIP). Traditionally the performance improvement plan (PIP), is not geared to improve performance but to push out or exclude the underperformer.

The performance improvement plan (PIP) is most effective when used as a personnel development tool, although the person impacted by the PIP does not often perceive it that way. The PIP should be reflective of the organization's culture, and when implemented and structured in a thoughtful way, it can serve as an effective shared-accountability tool.

The Traditional Way

We want to demonstrate that we are not suggesting the dismantling of systems of accountability. Sometimes the most helpful leadership approach will involve evaluation, such as in the example below, a case in which data helped create a sense of accountability.

> Daisy, a high school principal in an urban district in New York City, was considered a high performer. She had served in her role for three years, and some of her peers thought she was well-positioned for executive leadership. Based on many of the key performance indicators of the organization, Daisy and her team were on track to have unprecedented achievements in one of the most impoverished congressional districts in the United States. Daisy's struggles started when she voiced her intention to push her team to achieve academic targets. She wanted to move the needle on student test scores and similar data points, but she was unwilling to engage parents in an authentic way. Needless to say, this was not well received in a close-knit community that valued educational excellence. Also, her approach to student discipline became problematic as she increased suspensions primarily for minority boys while denying hot lunches to

students who violated the school's hierarchy of rules. The latter decisions were glaring signals of significant gaps in her ability and willingness to understand and be helpful as a leader. These actions resulted in a decrease in mission-driven actions for the entire team, and in many ways they did not have a positive impact on anyone's happiness.

Criticism

Criticism manifests itself in several ways. When someone is deemed a "poor performer," the person evaluating usually knows that feedback and support should be offered. However, giving feedback is known as one of the most challenging tasks leaders face, and consequently it is one they tend to avoid altogether. When employees underperform and their leaders are unable or unwilling to invest in building capacity, criticism ensues. Leaders share their criticism of employees with peers or with other stakeholder groups, rarely with the affected person. Because they can't (or choose not to) talk to their employee, they speak negatively about him or her. Lack of constructive feedback, feedback designed to help the employee develop, immediately causes additional problems. Criticism is usually

The Traditional Way

burdened with assumptions, innuendo, and surface-level investigation. Without a deeper look at the root causes of underachievement, the employee's performance – and the organization's bottom line –continue to suffer.

Criticism causes associates to experience a disconnect between their supervisor's perceptions and their actual performance. Take the case of Daisy. She and her supervisor disagreed about the perceived gaps in her competencies and ability. She believed in reaching the data targets by any means necessary. Her leaders believed that the "how" was important. Regardless, Daisy's supervisor utilized an empathetic and compassionate leadership approach, and criticism never entered the conversation. Like Daisy's supervisor, all good leaders know that criticism often results in defensiveness, which manifests itself in statements such as "you are not here enough to make a judgment," "you are only getting a snapshot of my performance," "you have never served in this role before," or "you don't understand what it really takes to perform this task." These types of disconnect and disagreement require a prudent response by the supervisor, one that encourages the employee to unpack the aforementioned statements and is anchored in a desire to understand his or her feelings. This is significant because if unresolved or unchecked, expressions of disapproval and ongoing disagreement between supervisors and employees usually have an adverse impact on the bottom line. Undesirable outcomes are the inevitable result of criticism, because any changes the employee might make to his or her work habits are likely to be inappropriate due to a lack of relevant feedback. Feedback rooted in uninformed criticism is rarely relevant. Consequently, criticism has an effect on the entire system by creating a cycle of low morale, disengagement, and decreased productivity.

Exclusion

Exclusion occurs shortly after evaluation and criticism have reared their ugly heads. In many organizations fewer than 10 percent of employees are respected for their perspective and insight. Conversely, members of the "elite" group are given the opportunity to have their voices heard and replicated throughout the organization. This practice stifles diversity and the benefits of having a variety of perspectives. In many instances exclusion occurs when only one group of

The Traditional Way

associates regularly engages with leaders. These extra touches result in this particular group being able to live the vision of the company's leadership. This leaves the other 90 percent of associates, many of whom may have a lot of value to add based on their untapped experience or expertise, regularly misaligned from the organizational vision. It is important to note that the top 10 percent is not chosen simply based on outcomes or performance. More often than not the selection process is based on favoritism, cronyism, or nepotism, and the work and true potential are secondary at best. By contrast, people in the "90 percent" group may have positive outcomes, but they are not considered to be part of the favored group and therefore are still left out, excluded from receiving accolades, incentives, and rewards. This practice causes large-scale disengagement and workplace dissatisfaction. Happiness suffers for everyone, including those in the chosen group.

Expulsion or Termination

Expulsion or termination is bound to be the next resort if and when other strategies don't result in desired outcomes.

The Power of Seven Second Chances

People get kicked out. Let's be clear, terminations are warranted at times. Let's revisit the Daisy story:

In response to Daisy's obvious gaps, her supervisor exhausted every opportunity to build capacity in her by offering daily coaching and out-of-district professional development, extending opportunities for her to connect with and engage the community, and even adding the offering of executive coaches. Ultimately, Daisy's refusal to adjust and be receptive to the supports provided by the organization resulted in her exhausting multiple opportunities to get it right. She was placed on a performance improvement plan with the hope of correcting and addressing her deficits and gaps in culturally responsive leadership. The plan was not created to kick Daisy out. It was intended to course-correct. Daisy did not respond favorably. She did not acknowledge that gaps in certain competencies existed, and she was terminated. It is important to note that Daisy was *not* terminated because she could not produce data to prove the organization's positive standing to its stakeholders. She was terminated because she failed to recognize and act upon the fact that at the end of every data

The Traditional Way

point, there are children. According to our friends at McGlore Elementary, "Happy children learn more!"

Daisy is a different situation. In general, people get kicked out without exhausting support and coaching opportunities. Talent management and recruitment strategies are compromised as a result. Organizations only concerned about the bottom line may fail to recognize that, basically, they are losing money for each hire they fail to retain. Onboarding new employees cost thousands of dollars. The cost to recruit and train a new associate is estimated to be on average $15,000 annually. For instance, in 2007, the National Commission on Teaching and America's Future (NCTAF) completed an 18-month study of the cost of teacher turnover in five school districts: Chicago Public Schools (IL), Milwaukee Public Schools (WI), Granville County Schools (NC), Jemez Valley Public Schools (NM), and Santa Rosa Public Schools (NM). The study also explored the cost in the recruitment, hiring, onboarding, and training or development of the teachers at the school and district level. The study revealed some variation in the cost findings because the school districts studied varied in size, demographics, and geographic location. In many school districts across the country, the aforementioned variations are compounded by the types of districts in question or by the school's onboarding or inducting programs. The one common finding was that regardless of the school or district, the cost of teacher turnover is substantial. The NCTAF utilized a Teacher Turnover Cost Calculator to arrive at the numbers. The calculator looked at the cost to districts and schools. According to the calculator, the cost to districts is steeped in two factors:

1. The district office expends resources during recruitment, hiring, onboarding, and training.
2. The schools incur costs when the candidates interview, are hired, processed and on-boarded, and professionally developed. The turnover cost calculator looked at the following levers to arrive at an average cost:
   - hiring incentives
   - administrative processing
   - induction and on-boarding
   - professional development

The Traditional Way

In addition to the two points from NCTAF, we have calculated the average financial cost per teacher at $8,000 - $15,000. This estimated cost does not include school-level costs, the cost to student-level learning, and other hidden costs.

What could be if schools spent a fraction of the aforementioned dollars on capacity building, training, and developing instead? Expulsion and termination also result in a perception of lack of stability within an organization. Even new generations of employees are attracted to job security as they enter the workforce and consider which professional pursuits to explore. Prospective employees look to termination stats as data points when deciding about where to work. Organizations perceived as quick to fire are not on the "best places to work" lists.

The cycle of evaluation, criticism, exclusion, and termination is ineffective. Not only is this approach ineffective, it is not solution-focused. We've done it this way forever. It does not work, yet we continue along the same path anyway. Albert Einstein stated that the definition of insanity is doing the same thing over and over and expecting a different result. We have the ability to stop the madness. In fact, we have seen examples in sports where an athlete hadn't been performing well, then went on to another team and found success. One might conclude that over time the athlete had simply learned from his or her mistakes and improved – pulled it together. What is as true or truer is that athletes, just like the people you lead, can improve their level of performance. There are many great examples of this being true when the people around them, especially their leaders, employ approaches designed to unearth the best in them as individuals.

What if we all embraced this mindset? What could be if, as leaders, we decided that it was a critical part of our role to appeal to the humanistic parts of each individual we lead? These are not rhetorical questions. We will ask you questions throughout the book. It is our hope that you will take time to reflect on them and truly answer.

What could be?

Regardless of how you just answered the question above, there is evidence-based research that suggests that if we adopt a different approach to the way we lead, we can experience some very tangible increases to our bottom line and improve our personal well-being.

Reflection Questions

1. What are the dangers of focusing on happiness? Of leaders? Of associates? Of community partners? Of clients, patients, children, or customers?

2. Think of a great experience you've had with an organization as an employee, community partner, or customer. How did you feel? What was the performance-management process like at that organization? If you did not work there, what do you imagine it was like?

3. In your view, how can accountability and associate happiness live together? Can you think of a few specific examples?

CHAPTER TWO THE TRICKLE-DOWN EFFECT

One specific benefit of exercising more empathy and compassion in leadership is the trickle-down effect. As we begin to demonstrate empathy and compassion, we will start to notice the same experience replicated throughout our organizations, with effects on our leaders, associates, clients, customers, and patrons. The field of education once again provides a good example. Student attendance and retention numbers improve when school leaders and teachers start to reduce the suspension rates of students across the country. Suspensions in education are the equivalent to terminations in business and industry; it's simply terminating your client, which in most cases makes little sense.

Allow us to share another example in educational leadership that pertains to all of us, even on its face. Still, our larger hope is that you will come to see yourself or your leadership approaches in this scenario and think about how the choice to follow the conventional cycle might not be helpful in the long run. Because the basics of adult learning (or lack thereof) as it relates to leadership is not much different

The Trickle Down Effect

across industries, there is a correlation between the lack of empathy in leadership to less than stellar organizational outcomes. In K-12 schools, this can be illustrated by focusing on student discipline and suspension rates. Unlike forty years ago, student-discipline data is thoroughly scrutinized today. This information is also now connected to the school-to-prison-pipeline epidemic. This connection highlights a simple but devastating chain reaction: the absence of empathetic and compassionate leadership leads to the removal of students from schools; this removal leads to school dropouts; school dropouts lead to the necessity to survive without the means to earn a living, which results in the criminalization of those who drop out.

To echo this, many economists and sociologists are continuously examining the connection to dropout rates and the economy. Remedies published in a UCLA study state that suspensions lead to increased dropouts. Over time, more dropouts mean reduced tax revenue and higher costs associated with crime, welfare, and healthcare. Dropouts also aggravate the war for talent in business and industry. Scalable empathetic and compassionate leadership may very well be the remedy to stem the continuous decline and ultimate failure of many of our schools and to help address America's talent shortage. Public safety and talent shortages are not the only issues, however. The UCLA study also found that in the 2015-2016 school year, 67,000 students dropped out of high school because of suspensions in 10th grade. Each high school dropout is costly to the nation. These staggering numbers represent approximately $35 billion in financial losses. If we were more intentional about retaining teachers and students, these rates would improve. Why is this significant? Because the United States has lost its preeminence in education when compared to other nations around the world, and consequently our country is falling behind according to several other leading indicators such as innovation. The chain reaction originating in a lack of empathetic and compassionate leadership in K-12 schools continues and metastasizes as these changes have a negative

The Trickle Down Effect

impact on the economy. Economist Lance Lochner found that every 1 percent increase in high school graduation rates is worth $1.4 billion to the U.S. economy. Public safety impact is just as important, if not more. As graduation rates increase, incidents of murder, aggravated assault, and motor vehicle theft decrease. Data and evidence linking high school graduation rates to types of leadership may be lacking, but empirical evidence and research cited in the book "Prisoners or Presidents" (written by Dr. Roberts) offer clear support for the "seven second chances" approach. "Seven second chances" is a philosophy anchored in empathetic and compassionate leadership, and it has resulted in a significant increase in outcomes in all industries.

Dr. Roberts was recruited to lead and turnaround one of the District of Columbia's lowest performing high schools; a school known for its rich history and community investment, but coined as a dangerous place and drop-out factory. When he inherited the school of approximately 1,000 students, he was informed that he was the 10th principal in 10 years, the school had an average daily student attendance that was hovering around 50%, the graduation rate was less than 50%, there were 299 arrest of students for crimes ranging from misdemeanors to felonies that included murder by the Metropolitan Police Department, ELA and Math scores on the state assessment were in the single digits. A survey of students revealed that their primary concern was the fact that they felt like they were the victims of inequitable treatment and they were not the recipients of the same opportunities as other students in other zip codes in the nation's capital.

While working as a principal in the District of Columbia Public schools, Dr. Roberts responded to the needs of the students and Anacostia community by embracing the seven second chance approach. In this assignment he learned that the school leader should focus on guaranteeing that students, teachers, and every stakeholder receive multiple chances to meet organizational goals and achieve the most helpful outcomes to the most people. He knew that his approach with his staff would also trickle down to the students. He realized that a seven second chance approach must include all stakeholders, especially the student. As a result of embracing this leadership philosophy which was

The Trickle Down Effect

anchored in empathetic and compassionate leadership, the school boasted the following data at the end of Dr. Roberts' four years at the helm: 20% increase in the graduation rate of seniors, more than 25% increase in the average daily attendance of students, 5% and 8% increases in ELA and Math assessments respectively. The number of arrest the first year was reduced from 299 to less than 30. The number of students applying to and being accepted to colleges and universities was over 90% of the graduating seniors, with several students receiving the most prestigious lucrative post-secondary scholarships that included two Gates Millennium Scholarships. A part of Dr. Roberts and his leadership team's approach was for everyone to become conversant with, and provide teacher, staff, and student with multiple opportunities to succeed. We know this statement might seem a bit anemic in such a high-need environment like Anacostia. Rest assured, it is not! It is the lynchpin for everything we profess in the remainder of this work.

Today, we regard that it is the school's leadership that must make every effort to gather pertinent information about all students in order to make informed decisions to best meet each student's needs. Every student, regardless of academic deficits, disciplinary history, or criminal record, should be allowed to enroll and given multiple opportunities for success and achievement. Every school and district leadership team should encourage every adult and other stakeholders to demonstrate an understanding of the needs or suffering of each student and adult. Such encouragement should include taking the necessary action to actually do something to alleviate the suffering. As a result, the outcomes experienced are

- improvement in average daily attendance,
- improved student academic performance,
- reduction in incidents of student discipline/suspension rates,
- an increase in teacher retention and engagement, and
- significant increases in student graduation rates.

According to Education Week, the most common causes of low graduation rates among high school students in the United States are: poor academic performance, poverty, disciplinary problems, and constant absenteeism. Maria O'Cadiz, a contributing writer for Education Week, has pointed out that, just as it happens with other social problems, students from poor economic backgrounds and minorities are disproportionally represented when it comes to low graduation rates, as they tend to drop out of high school more regularly than other groups. According to the Pew Partnership, completion rates among Asian and White students stands at 77 and 75 percent respectively, higher than the national average of 68.8 percent. Conversely, among African American, Hispanic, and American-Indian students, the percentage is about 50 percent. The truth is, most students from minority ethnicities attend underfunded, underserved, and underrated schools where accountability is diluted by a tolerance for underachievement, which in turn perpetuates the status quo of apathy and failure. But even "failing" schools can have leadership that emphasizes empathy and compassion; leadership where there is intentionality and a commitment to understand the needs of students and their communities, leadership that makes every effort to mitigate impediments to success.

These kinds of schools, like Anacostia High School in Washington, D.C., have experienced significant increases in graduation rates and other measures of student success.

Trickle-Down Effect

The leaders are the catalyst. Their behaviors create the outcomes we ultimately see on the ground.

Education	Industry	Military	Religious Institution	Healthcare
Superintendent/ Principals	CEO	Captain/ Lieutenant	Pastor	Providers
Teachers	Employees	Sergeants	Deacons	Staff
Students/ Families	Customers	Privates	Parishioners	Patients

We believe that all leaders can be great – not some, but all. It is time for us to behave as if we believe that leaders can be made. Their ability to perform in their roles is not cast in stone. We can develop that ability, and we can begin today to lead like we understand that developing leadership muscle is foundational to our roles. People will walk into our organizations every day with coaching and development

The Trickle Down Effect

needs. In some cases, we identify that the needs are great. However, once we have hired an associate, we have to embrace the reality that every person has a coaching need. This is not an evaluation; it is a fact. Every person can increase his or her capacity in some area. While some organizations can hire the best and ditch the rest, most of us have to work on our workplace culture. In conjunction with culture, we have to teach our leaders the empathetic and compassionate approach to leadership, because there is an "in the meantime" experience. What do we mean? Every year we learn about the companies that make the "best places to work" lists. We all aspire to be like them – all of us. But what do you do in the meantime if you aren't on that list? What do you do in the meantime if your organization is on that list, but there are pockets in your company, school, or healthcare facility where people are suffering? We know this is true. Empathetic and compassionate leadership is the short-term answer and the long-term solution. We don't have to be surprised when our associates and leaders don't meet our expectations. We can embrace it instead and step confidently into our ability to develop whatever might be missing. Empathy and compassion will get us there. If we are honest, we can all recall a time when we, personally or professionally, had a skill gap, and someone understood and helped us. Now it's our turn. How do you want leaders to treat you? How would you like them to approach you when you have missed a deadline? Remember how you personally feel in these situations. Then find the desire to be helpful to others in the same way that you would have wanted to be helped. This is the pure definition of empathy and compassion.

This is not a softening approach. It is recognition that people are more inclined to demonstrate an increased investment when they are treated as individuals and not only as contributors on the assembly line. Every person should be treated as a human being and as more than a pawn to achieve the organizations bottom-line. However, with a foundation of accountability, treating people with respect and dignity will result in meeting the performance targets anyway.

Leaders who are constantly making decisions steeped in intellectual capacity instead of emotional intelligence do not

The Trickle Down Effect

get the same return on investment from a personnel and human resources standpoint. Empathetic and compassionate organizations and teams understand that employee engagement is incredibly important in achieving bottom-line and organizational success. Gallup states that an engaged employee is more likely to stay and will give discretionary effort. In spite of the many technological advances we witness every day, 90 percent of organizations still rely on people to get work done. People like to be complimented, cajoled, and rewarded. This is why we are focused on what inspires people. Empathetic and compassionate leadership is a critical component of leading people in inspirational ways. For this reason, we believe it is imperative that we establish a baseline for what the words empathy and compassion mean as we will use them throughout this text.

<u>Empathy</u> *(I look at you and see me.)*
Empathy in leadership happens when individuals who are in a position of influence make every effort to understand the position and circumstances of the people being led and make decisions that align to their needs. Empathy requires that I understand your issue; it requires the ability to relate. An

empathetic leader will see a person struggling or suffering and will recall a similar time, event, or circumstance is his or her own life.

<u>Compassion</u> *(I don't see myself in you. I see you as a distinct person, but I want to do all I can to help you suffer less.)*
Sometimes it's easier to start with what something *isn't*. Compassionate leadership is not sympathy. It also isn't the softening of a leadership approach. Compassion is (1) realizing that a person is suffering, and (2) having the desire to make it better for that person. Compassion is an internal feeling, which is why in our work situations we prefer to suppress compassion. For years we have been told that it is more appropriate in work situations to suppress what the heart feels and focus merely on the facts of situations. True compassion requires just the opposite – that you allow your heart to burst wide open. Compassion is expressing true and genuine concern for a peer or direct report. You look directly into the suffering of another person and feel motivated to relieve the suffering. Compassion is concerning yourself with what a colleague may have endured and allowing his or her perspective to be important during initial conversations,

before passing judgment. Does relieving a person's suffering make you "soft"? Does it mean that you won't approach difficult conversations? We believe that direct, clear messages, as well as having the courage to tackle those conversations that matter the most, do not cause suffering, but they can, in fact, relieve suffering.

When we mention empathetic and compassionate leadership, many people immediately think about their lower performers. If you fall into this category, we ask that you consider a new approach. Avoid thinking about the "worst" in others and focus on the best in others. What if we were suggesting empathy and compassion toward your best performers? Would you object? Likely not! We ask that you follow us on this journey as we invite you to consider the idea that everyone deserves empathy and compassion *and* that behaving this way does not come at the expense of excellence in leadership.

Reflection Questions

1. What are the implications of shifting the organizational focus from fear and force-based change efforts to a fair-based approach?
2. When you consider your organization's current policies and practices, what are some shifts you should make in order to minimize the negative impact of terminations of any kind (i.e., suspending a student, cancelling a client, firing an employee)?
3. How can you or your organization address the notion that empathetic and compassionate leadership erode or diminish accountability?

CHAPTER THREE LEADING EMPATHETICALLY AND COMPASSIONATELY

We would be remiss if we did not acknowledge a common misconception in conversations about empathy and compassion in leadership, a misconception related to sympathy. To be clear, sometimes sympathy is called for in leadership, and we can offer an example from our own lives. In our working relationship, there was a crucial point at which all three – empathy, compassion, and sympathy – were necessary in order to maintain the relationship and build ties that could withstand the challenges of the incredibly important work we each do every day. It was 2014, and Dr. Roberts' dad died after suffering through a lengthy illness. At the same time, we were starting to do some new and important work together. Dr. Roberts had also changed jobs and moved in anticipation of his father's passing. We are colleagues and easily follow each other's leadership. People are rarely willing to allow a leader to emerge based what is needed in a particular situation. This unwillingness is usually the result of an evolving relationship. To be clear, the working relationship between us had not reached this evolutionary point yet. This is an important point, because often people mistakenly believe that trust has to be at an all-time high in order to practice empathy and compassion. In fact, you can choose to trust the empathetic and compassionate approach even when you might not naturally choose to trust an individual or group. Below we offer a simple explanation to help you delineate the difference between sympathy, empathy and compassion.

The Situation. Dr. Roberts' dad has died. Nicole and Dr. Roberts have important work to do. Dr. Roberts appears to be fully available to continue working, and Nicole wants to continue the work.

Sympathy. Nicole knows that death can cause grief to show up in various ways. Nicole feels bad about Dr. Roberts' father's death and about the fact that Dr. Roberts is grieving.

Empathy. Nicole looks at Dr. Roberts' situation, and she recalls the deaths of her own father and mother (*relating*). She remembers how she felt when she was in a situation like Dr. Roberts's (*understanding*).

Compassion. Being motivated by empathy, Nicole's heart is open. She cares (*caring increases motivation*) about his well-being. She wants to help Dr. Roberts (*wanting to help is critical*). She has a conversation with Dr. Roberts about what would be helpful and uncovers that work is a source of relief and escape. So, for him, she continues to focus on the work. She also finds that he is a private person who likes to work through personal matters alone. With that, she makes it clear that she is available but does not push

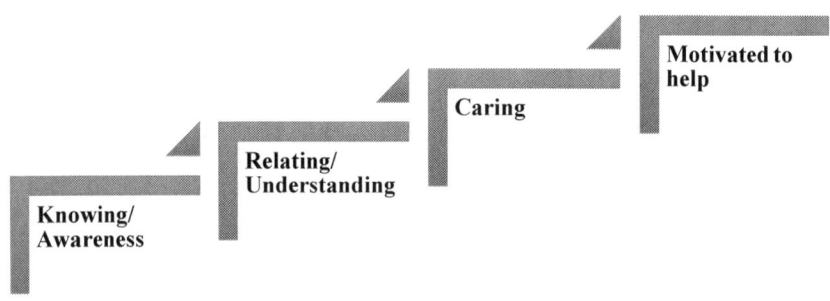

The key is seeing that the helpful action will not be the same for everyone. What would be helpful to one person may not

be helpful to another. Empathy and compassion require that we do not try to treat everyone the same; they require that we treat everyone looking to motivate the actions that would help the most. We define "helpful" as that which results in the greatest positive impact on the most people. A combination of empathy and compassion in leadership is a moral approach; however, this is not only a moral obligation. Empathy and compassion in leadership will increase the leader's engagement or happiness, and it will also increase the engagement or happiness of his or her employees. Our associates don't require that we feel sorry for them or that we sympathize with their situations. After all, although feeling sorry for people is appropriate in some situations, feeling sorry has not done much to help anyone. By contrast, if you have the ability to relate to others (*empathy*), and when that relational tie helps you to recall a time in your life when you experienced a similar situation, your understanding is helpful. In fact, your understanding can lead to the desire to relieve the frustration, barriers, suffering, etc. of your colleague. Understanding is helps you do what you can within your power to improve the situation. Behaving like this is morally right, but it is also solidly good for business.

Leading Empathetically and Compassionately

What if the people you work with every day were giving discretionary effort? What could you accomplish if intent to stay were high and you weren't constantly retraining due to turnover?

A simple strategy we suggest when people struggle with being empathetic and compassionate is to replace the words "empathy" and "compassion" with the words "understanding" and "motivated to help." When people offer us scenarios like, "Are you saying I should be empathetic and compassionate with this leader?" The answer is clearer when we rephrase the question to "Are you saying I should be understanding and motivated to help this leader?" Often the answer is a resounding "YES!"

Leading with empathy and compassion has its associated pitfalls. One of them is compassion fatigue. Compassion fatigue is defined as having an indifference to charitable appeals on behalf of those who are suffering, and it is experienced as a result of the frequency or number of such appeals. In other words, in some professions the number of times a leader is required to be "understanding and motivated to help" can seem limitless. In those instances, leaders run the risk of losing the ability to care. Compassion fatigue is worse when leadership is lacking. According to the Compassion Fatigue Awareness Project, when compassion fatigue is present, the mistrust associates feel toward management is not unfounded, and it results in negative organizational behaviors like high absenteeism, in-fighting, failure to meet goals, reluctance to change, and many other detrimental characteristics. The good news is that the leader does matter! Leaders can help ensure that associates

- create a culture whereby people are kind to themselves and others
- communicate and celebrate the development path
- are present to members of their staff
- honor boundaries
- have rejuvenation time

The natural human desire is to be appreciated and celebrated. In his book "The Pursuit of Purpose," the late Myles Munroe, pastor of the Bahamas Faith Ministries International, often sermonized, "Every human has the innate desire to be appreciated and celebrated." Using systems of evaluation threaten this basic principle. We are inviting leaders everywhere to adopt the idea that we each have the ability to interrupt the cycle at evaluation and disrupt a leadership approach that has proven ineffective. In fact, we assert that you can celebrate the fact that every person has a development need. Once a developmental gap in ability or performance is identified, instead of criticizing, it would behoove leaders in organizations to inspire and empower their personnel to improve.

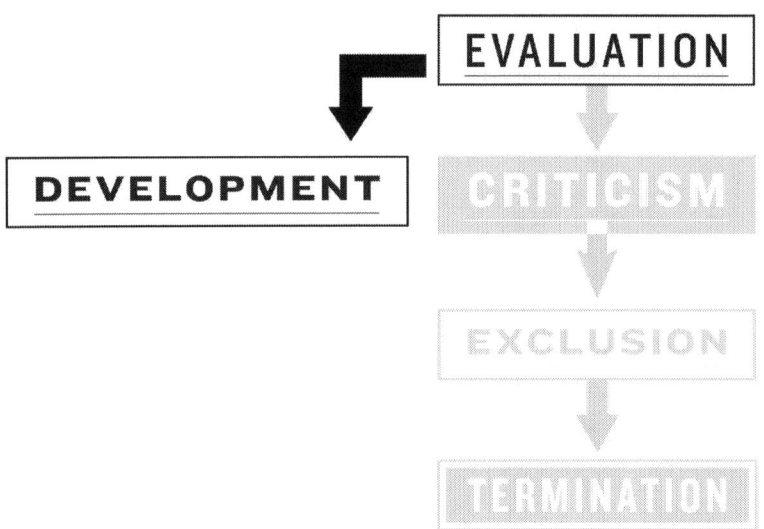

Reflection Questions

1. Take some time to reflect: Can you recall a situation or circumstance that caused you to pivot towards an empathetic and compassionate approach in your personal or professional pursuit? What was the impact?
2. How is trust within the team factored into the culture of your organization? What about trust in leadership?
3. What preemptive action or approach can leaders or organizations take in order to mitigate the inevitable onset of compassion fatigue?

CHAPTER FOUR INTERRUPTING THE CYCLE USING THE SEVEN SECOND CHANCE APPROACH

While transitioning from District of Columbia Public Schools Dr. Roberts was charged with, among other deliverables, transforming the organizational culture on several fronts, one of which was teacher and staff retention. To this end, he focused on investigating the reasons why people were not staying with the organization and the factors that the adults and the children who were leaving had in common. One possible solution was to create a culture of personnel support geared toward increasing retention rates among faculty and staff.

Special attention was given to whether the employees and students who were separated had been given opportunities to improve. The primary question was whether they had been invested in the mission and vision of the organization and whether the leadership had cultivated the commitment of these adults and students. A second question was whether those who had left had experienced empathy and compassion during their time with the organization, and whether those moments had been in conflict with the achievement of bottom-line goals. Essentially, the question was whether or not the affected individuals had benefitted from seven second chances.

The "seven second chance" approach is simple but not always easy. The approach calls for leaders to be incredibly forgiving at the evaluation stage. Once a leader has identified a potential issue, he or she is invited to grant another chance to the offender – whoever he or she might be. This second chance is not simply offered once but rather seven times! Offering seven second chances is, in essence, giving 14 chances to an individual after evaluation. It is an interruption in the performance management process. This approach is critically important because it forces leaders to be creative with the development process and avoid the vicious cycle that leads to expulsions and terminations. On the contrary, this approach creates an environment whereby everyone knows that he or she will be given multiple opportunities to get it right; it is a demonstration of leadership that is motivated to help – it is compassionate.

Interrupting the Cycle

Why *seven* second chances? Where did this seeming absurdity come from? The genesis of the "seven second chances" leadership philosophy is connected to four strands:

1. The understanding of and appreciation for the power of the number seven. In ancient cultures, the Hebrew culture included, the number seven is associated with completion and perfection. Leaders and practitioners who embrace the "seven second chances" philosophy invest in the complete person and not just in their intellectual capacity and their ability to contribute to the organization's or team's bottom line.

2. During Dr. Roberts' tenure as a turnaround school leader, the team of adults in the building was encouraged to provide every student that was being considered for discipline, especially harsh discipline, at least 14 chances (7x2) to "get it right." In response to frustrations, adults are likely to keep copious notes on failures, unmet expectations, and rule violations by students and adults, all this with the intent of removing "troublemakers" from the organization or team as they exhaust a too-easily-met

quota of failures. The "seven second chances" approach encourages and forces the leader or practitioner to exhaust every effort to coach, and build capacity in the affected adult or student.

3. The number seven has been used in profound ways in the Bible and other stories and religious writings originating in ancient cultures. The following are references that align to the "seven second chances" leadership stance and philosophy:

Matthew 18:21-22 – Peter came to him and said ... Lord, how often shall my brother sin against me, and I forgive him? Till seven times? Jesus's response was, I say not unto thee, until seven times, but until seventy times seven.

Mark 6:41 – Taking the **five loaves and the two fish** and looking up to heaven, he gave thanks and broke the loaves. Then he gave them to his disciples to distribute to the people.

2nd Kings 5:1-10 – Naaman was a decorated, respected commander of the Syrian Army. However, he had

Leprosy. Elisha told him to **dip 7 times** in the River Jordan and he would be healed.

The number seven felt incredibly important.

Some leaders can serve as exemplars or models of how forgiveness and empathy may be applied also to personal pursuits. The Dalai Lama is an example of one such leader. The teachings of the Dalai Lama, although often at odds with Western culture on the topics of empathy and compassion and never given as much press as other approaches, have guided transformational leadership approaches and resulted in the success of many contemporary organizations.

In chapter two, we explored several definitions of compassion. The one we embrace comes from Tibetan scholar Thurpten Jinpa. Jinpa, better known as the English translator for the Dalai Lama, defines compassion as a mental state whereby someone expresses concern for the pain, circumstance, and suffering of others, and is willing to take action to relieve that suffering. As a reminder, this definition includes

1. a cognitive component: "I understand you."

2. an affective component: "I feel you."
3. a motivational component: "I want to help you."

Leaders who commit to understanding the circumstance of those whom they lead and serve and are willing to alleviate those circumstances to benefit the people and organization are practitioners of empathetic and compassionate leadership. Empathetic and compassionate leaders are willing to give those with whom they come into contact multiple opportunities to get it right. Similarly, the leadership philosophy of seven second chances has guided the work of many school leaders nationally as they achieve unprecedented success in student discipline, teacher retention, and student academic achievement. This philosophy is also aligned to the practices of empathetic and compassionate leadership.

Why will empathetic and compassionate leaders transform the educational landscape?

In the arena of K-12 education, the United States has lost its preeminence among the developed countries of the world.

Interrupting the Cycle

Politicians, education gurus and pundits, and policy makers have responded with education policy measures and laws that seem to evolve with each presidential election cycle. These measures, none of which has highlighted or proposed empathetic or compassionate leadership as a strategy, have included the following:

- Lyndon Johnson's Elementary and Secondary Education Act (ESA, 1965), which touted the idea that education was the tool that would eventually win the "war on poverty." The legislation pressed for equal education and access to quality education for all.

- "The Nation at Risk" was Ronald Regan's 1983 report calling for educational reform. The document was grounded in the belief that the U.S., which had enjoyed unchallenged dominance in commerce, industry, science, and technological innovation, was being overtaken by competitors throughout the world. The report attributed this American decline to the fact that our K-12 and post-secondary educational institutions were being eroded.

- Bill Clinton's Goals 2000 was signed into law in 1994, and it asserted, "Every student can learn." The legislation was intended to abolish the distinction that put academic learning and skill development in competition with one another. Instead, the law pointed out that states have the authority to formulate plans to engage every student in educational programs to make them both learned and competitive.

- George Bush's No Child Left Behind (NCLB, 2001) is said to be the most sweeping educational-reform legislation since Lyndon Johnson's 1965 ESEA. The law increased accountability and testing, and it promised to get every student to achieve at unprecedented levels.

- Barack Obama's Every Student Succeed Act (ESSA, 2015) promised that the federal government would relinquish decision-making on education policy and practice in favor of states and districts.

The aforementioned policies have one thing in common: they all magnify the idea that school leaders must be tough, hard-nosed, no-nonsense change agents with high IQs to regurgitate the current educational vernacular and produce the right responses during interviews. One unintended or intended consequence of placing this expectation on school leaders is that it created a particular atmosphere in schools; it perpetuated the "us against them" dynamic (i.e., teachers and staff against school leaders), and in this dynamic no one is practicing empathy or compassion.

It is important to note that practicing empathy and compassion has to include culturally responsive leadership. At present, the aforementioned legislative policies create strict accountability measures but fail to provide any guidance on culturally responsive leadership. Both the NCLB and ESSA, the federal education policies between 2001 and 2016 are perpetuating the education policy status quo without any obvious adjustment or guidance for those in the K-12 education arena to follow. This is unacceptable because there has been a dramatic demographic shift in America; and school leaders and educators must be skilled to handle those shifts. Interestingly, one group that has made the shift in their practices or philosophy is politicians. They have strategically made adjustments in their political campaign strategies in order to secure the votes of constituents in Black and Hispanic communities. What is fascinating and equally disappointing, is that the most obvious dramatic demographic shift has occurred in the K-12 education arena. This shift is not a problem at all; the real problem lies in the fact that our education systems, curricula, pedagogical, and leadership practices have not adjusted to accommodate the shifts. It is even apparent that, unlike politicians, educators are not even faking empathy and compassion towards those who would respond favorably to a culturally responsive approach. Empathy and compassion are the foundational competencies of culturally responsive pedagogy and leadership. A clear example can be found by revisiting the United States 2016 presidential election campaign. During the campaign, several candidates did excellent jobs of pretending to empathize with women and the Black and Hispanic communities. However, there were times when the winning candidate publicly and blatantly expressed his disgust and disdain for those two ethnic groups and for women. This disgust and disdain manifested itself in condescending, discriminatory, and prejudicial behaviors towards them. However, the post-election polls showed that this pretense of empathy resulted in Hispanics, "the Blacks," and women casting their votes for him. As a result, a leader who could be seen as one of the nation's least empathetic candidates won the presidential election. What if leaders expressed empathy and compassion? Could it be that the expression would lead to the eventual outcome of being empathetic and compassion? It is our hope that this could be true for the president of the United States of America. Let's be clear, we are in no way encouraging the practice of inauthentic leadership. We strongly believe that inauthenticity in leadership quickly erodes and diminishes ones professional, intellectual, and street credibility. However, the practice of "acting as if" as coined by Alan Deustchman in the book Change or Die has been shown to result in changed behaviors.

Teachers, school leaders, health care providers, and other service industry workers in our nation experience this dynamic of inauthentic displays of empathy and compassion firsthand. Teachers frequently express feeling anxiety after a supervisor visits the classroom and observes their lessons.

The wait time between the visit and the feedback is stressful. This stress trickles down to the students. And what is the source of the stress? It starts with evaluation, or the perception of always being evaluated; however, evaluation alone is not the cause. After a classroom, school, or plant visit, teachers, school leaders, or plant managers fully expect to receive feedback, and in some instances, even criticism. We humbly submit that, although not a panacea, intentionally creating and cultivating organizational cultures where the new normal is empathetic and compassionate leadership will mitigate the negative atmosphere that exists within many organizations. Leaders can assess performance without causing stress if they approach the process with the intention to understand and help in whatever way is needed. This kind of leadership shares accountability for success and failure with team members. Setting clear and explicit expectations on shared accountability does not mean that one must become dictatorial or a hard-nosed leader. The kind of leadership that prioritizes people over the bottom line results in increased morale, high stakeholder investment, and high retention rates among the most impactful employees.

Interrupting the Cycle

Have you ever wondered if it's possible to lead and teach with empathy and compassion when you may have never experienced that kind of leadership? Leaders often lead the way they were led. So even with the best of intentions, these leaders' personal experiences create their reality. When it comes to providing their direct reports (teachers and staff), as well as their students, with doses of compassionate and empathetic leadership, not only do they not have the experience, but the culture of the organization may not support it. We have often wondered about the necessary steps to lead empathetically and compassionately in these environments. There is a misconception that those who focus on leading with empathy and compassion are often reluctant or incapable of enforcing strict systems of accountability. It is critical for people in leadership positions and authority to balance empathy and compassion with accountability.

Within organizations there are frequently strict accountability structures in place, but the question often asked is; how is this culture impacting the health of the organization, the team or its people? We recommend the creation of a culture that reminds everyone that mistakes are allowed. This is significant because knowing that mistakes are allowed builds a foundation for innovation and risk-taking. These are core values of some of the most successful organizations.

Although presidential debates and campaigns are not necessarily the yardstick against which to measure good leadership, during a U.S. election the media will have us believe that good leaders are not "soft"; they are "tough," "results-oriented," "relentless," and "intellectually gifted." Leaders who prioritize benevolence over the bottom line have no place in our institutions. Leadership that is cerebral and has a head orientation speaks to one's IQ; leadership that is empathetic and compassionate has a heart orientation but is not what attracts recruiters. This is just one formulation of a common misconception about leadership: many people believe that leaders must be tough in order to transform organizations, and that leading with the heart is the antithesis of tough, goal-oriented leadership. This false narrative has resulted in many organizational cultures in contemporary society being flooded with an orientation that lacks empathy and compassion.

Leadership consists in being placed in a position of authority over one or several individuals in order to attain a goal. Goal attainment usually requires the leader to act with a sense of urgency. Essentially, this results in an attitude that says, "Let's get it done now! If you do not demonstrate the competencies that we need, you will be replaced!" Empathetic and compassionate leaders are willing to exhaust every opportunity to build capacity in the people they lead and with whom they serve.

Leaders who embark on the path of "seven second chances" leadership are often challenged by peers who ask, "How many opportunities are you willing to give someone to improve his or her craft, to exercise effective [fill in the blank], or to get it right?" Our response is consistently anchored in the power of seven second chances. The power of seven second chances espouses that an excellent exercise in empathetic and compassionate leadership is a willingness to give every individual not just seven chances, but rather to give two chances, *seven times over*. The thinking is rooted in the belief that most adults and children will be successful if they are given 14 chances to improve. In his best-selling book "Blink," Malcolm Gladwell argues that it takes 10,000 hours of practice on a skill to achieve expert status. We submit that it takes 14 chances for individuals to appreciate that their leaders are willing to allow for mistakes and embrace course corrections. People will make mistakes if they are taking chances and building new capabilities, and even when they are leveraging their strengths. People who are afraid of repercussions will not try much; their risk-taking ability is compromised.

In too many instances, we are conditioned to believe that giving individuals seven second chances to succeed is soft and makes us vulnerable. Companies that are willing to ingrain the seven second chances into their culture must do so with their leaders modeling why this approach is important. The leaders of many successful organizations prioritize the importance of empathy and compassion. One such organization once had a vacancy for a senior leadership position that came with tremendous benefits and a very competitive compensation package. Reportedly, one Friday

Interrupting the Cycle

morning a highly qualified and sought-after candidate arrived at 6:30 a.m. for an 8 a.m. interview. He was impeccably dressed in a designer suit and was well prepared. As he entered the building, he accidentally tripped over the mop bucket and spilled the water. The custodian, who happened to be wiping walls a few feet away, turned around and apologized effusively, to which the highly sought-after candidate responded, "What stupid person would leave a mop bucket behind a closed door?" He then walked away angrily muttering about his $2,000 pair of shoes, now soiled. The clerk at the front desk intervened with an apology and offered to take the candidate to the penthouse suite that he would occupy should he have a successful interview. He arrived at the penthouse suite, where he was met by plush, expensive furniture and an unrivaled view of the Hudson River in Manhattan. He reviewed the folder of information with his name on it that sat on the table, and he saw that the annual salary for the position he sought exceeded half a million dollars and came with fringe benefits including a driver, company car, and two paid overseas vacations per year. This was his dream job. Twenty minutes later he was summoned to a conference room, where he thoroughly impressed senior executives and board members. One interviewer said that he was by far the most dynamic and impressive candidate they had interviewed, and that he would likely be the last. In the same breath, the interviewer cautioned that ultimately the CEO would be making the hiring decision. The candidate was told the CEO, whom he would be meeting shortly, had watched the interview on closed-circuit video. At that very moment, a slim, well-dressed, charismatic gentleman walked in from an adjacent room. He sat down slowly, the word "CEO" inscribed in golden letters on the table tent in front of him. The gentleman now sitting at the CEO's desk was the same person whose bucket had been kicked over by the interviewee. The CEO echoed the sentiments of his colleagues regarding the astute and brilliant nature of the interviewee. He also told him that his actions earlier in the day had been the antithesis of the company's core value. When the candidate asked what that core value was, the CEO replied, "We pride ourselves on empathetic and compassionate interactions."

Empathy and compassion are ideas often associated with altruism and benevolence but never looked at as being an added value to an organization's daily operational excellence strategy. Many organizations, both successful and unsuccessful ones, struggle with retaining the best, brightest, and most effective. In chapter one we mentioned Zappos as an example of a company that prioritizes the happiness of its people and has built its success on that foundation. Having the freedom to explore, try on, and try out new skills is critical to building the cultures we all admire, and it requires empathy and compassion.

Reflection Questions

1. How can leaders and their teams balance the strict policies and requirements of legislation with the necessity and demands of an empathetic and compassionate leadership approach?
2. Is it possible to lead and teach with empathy and compassion if that's not how you have been led or guided?
3. What are some challenges or pitfalls that might accompany the "seven second chance" approach? What are risk-mitigation strategies you might employ to overcome those challenges?

CHAPTER FIVE
SEVEN GUIDANCE POINTS TO LEADING WITH EMPATHY AND COMPASSION

We have identified seven guidance points to leading with empathy and compassion.

1. **Epitomize selfless leadership.** The leaders who build strong teams, teams in which every team member has a high level of investment, are those who continuously demonstrate a genuine interest in people. One example of this kind of interest is to distribute a weekly communication in which all members of the team or organization are strongly encouraged to introduce themselves to someone else, especially a student, patient, client, or customer whose name they do not know, or with whom they do not normally interact. During these interactions consider investigating personal areas that you normally would avoid or overlook, such as future plans, place of residence, living situation. Additionally, genuinely compliment colleagues daily. Essentially, be

intentional about developing strong and authentic relationships without thinking about the benefit to you.

2. **Rise above personal attacks/criticism.** In response to personal criticism and attacks, former First Lady of the United States Michelle Obama once said, "When [people] go low, we go high." At all costs, do not respond to personal attacks, ridicule, or criticism from peers or any other stakeholder. Leaders with a high level of emotional intelligence will respond by rising above the fray, even when the attacks are intended to marginalize and cause hurt. Yes, people may at times respond negatively to various pressures, whether it be not meeting a target, or feeling threatened by a leader's poise during the storm of apparent mission failure. These kinds of responses don't need to be reciprocated. An empathetic and compassionate leader who embodies the philosophy of the "seven second chances" approach is able to face criticism and redirect the attacker or critic toward the team or organization's mission.

3. **Take ownership.** Leaders who anchor their team's work in a theory of action that highlights shared responsibility and shared accountability will inevitably encourage individual responsibility for failures and shortcomings. The leader who practices the "seven second chances" approach encourages reflection and personal responsibility without exerting the pressures of evaluation yet without abandoning the practice of evaluation either. Teams and organizations that encourage members to take ownership for failures and success alike are likely to have high morale and increased organizational retention amongst members. Demonstrating and modeling vulnerability are critically important behaviors for a leader, because people are more likely to trust leaders who openly admit their own mistakes.

4. **Believe that people have the best intentions.** As the saying goes among teachers, "parents send us their best students every day." Essentially, educators do not assume that parents keep their best and brightest children at home and send their most challenging ones to schools to

be educated. Similarly, in leadership we should demonstrate a belief that the people in our organizations are committed and doing their best within given circumstances. When members of an organization are not meeting its standards, the empathetic and compassionate approach encourages leaders to identify what might be the interference or impediment and to help remove the barrier through coaching. Empathetic leaders avoid thinking people are "out to get them," incompetent, lazy, stupid (or not as smart as they are), or that they left their better selves at home or at previous jobs. They take the time to find out why what they believe to be a simple task is not being executed well by someone else. They find out more about why people behave the way they do to help put them back on the right track. Leaders who embrace the "seven second chances" approach exercise empathetic leadership and balance it with shared accountability. To do so, engage in a conversation that gets to the bottom of what the person in question feels about the task, what constitutes an excellent execution of efforts, and what the person truly believes to be his or her role in achieving an excellent outcome.

5. **Scalable leadership equals supporting people's trajectory for growth and success.** The adage "We want our children to exceed the achievements of their parents" is a solid yardstick for leadership. Self-actualized leaders are those who exercise empathy and compassion in their work and in so doing create opportunities for other people to exceed their achievements. These leaders are what may be called the "trajectory visionaries." Like an excellent teacher who has the ability to see his students' potential, a teacher who does not judge and who educates based not on who students are now but rather on who they may become, leaders who embrace the seven second chances approach and empathetic leadership see possibilities and potential in every employee under their tutelage. The major difference between empathetic leaders and a more traditional leader is that they recognize this potential and are intentional about coaching, encouraging, and supporting team members to help them achieve more, improve their own careers, and fulfill their aspirations. This is a sure way to scale leadership and overall organization improvement.

6. **Be fast to listen and slow to speak.** A common reminder issued by many mothers, including each of our own, is that people have two ears and one mouth for a reason. The reason, of course, is that we should listen more than we speak. Empathetic and compassionate leaders never aspire to be the dominant voice in the room or at the table; they listen more than they speak even in critical situations demanding immediate solutions and answers. Rather than jump to premature conclusions, blame others, or shirk their responsibility regarding the situation, empathetic and compassionate leaders remain poised, composed, and anchored in a solutions-oriented stance. As a leader in an era of "urgency for results," avoid making any evaluative conclusions about other leaders when they are not meeting their targets or goals before the first 60 to 90 days. Although this idea runs counter to the "sense of urgency" that plagues most contemporary organizations and teams, conducting a deep analysis and gathering the appropriate information before speaking on the performance or evaluating and criticizing is simply prudent.

7. **Avoid quick fixes.** Organizations that desire fast solutions are almost always in reform and reorganization mode. "We have to operate with a sense of urgency" is just another way of saying, "We need a quick fix." We have rarely seen instances where the "sense of urgency" approach resulted in sustainable improvements and the achievement of the bottom line. Sure, the empathetic and compassionate approach requires patience and a focus that is often unprecedented. The payoff is that it builds teams that learn to exhibit a high level of emotional intelligence. The "sense of urgency" style is often impulsive, and it uses a headstrong (intelligence quotient), hard-nosed approach that dangles evaluation and a performance matrix over the heads of employees. Conversely, the approach that taps into empathetic and compassionate leadership encourages both the leader and the team to be objective and to keep their emotions in check during difficult times.

These seven guidance points are not the panacea or an exhaustive list of attributes that empathetic and compassionate leaders exhibit. They are the seven points in which "seven second chances" leaders anchor their approach. The leader or practitioner who demonstrates an affinity for the "seven second chance" approach to work is one who embraces and encourages empathy and compassion as a necessary tool to achieve the organization's or team's bottom line.

Guidance Points

Reflection Questions

1. Which of the seven strategies do you exhibit on a daily basis, and why do you believe it is important to outcomes?
2. The authors suggest that a self-actualized leader is one who demonstrates empathy and compassion. Do you agree or disagree? Why?
3. Is it possible for leaders without an empathetic and compassionate orientation to recognize ability, potential, and capacity in every person? If so, how? If not, why not?

CHAPTER SIX THE PRICE-ROBERTS MODEL

From the seven guidance points of empathetic and compassionate leadership, hopefully you can see that the approach does not only include the actions of the leader but also the actions he or she encourages and inspires in his or her team. The Price-Roberts Model includes an approach to self-development that is absent a performance improvement plan in the traditional sense. The model is not an external approach to correct but rather an internal, reflective approach that every member of the team is encouraged to embrace. This adoption emerges not from a punitive and evaluative position but rather from the position that every person has potential, strengths to be celebrated, and the ability to have an impact on his or her own happiness; it emerges from the belief that we all have a shared accountability to a larger purpose, to ourselves, to our team members, to our students, patients, clients or customers, and to our organizations' missions.

Price-Roberts Model

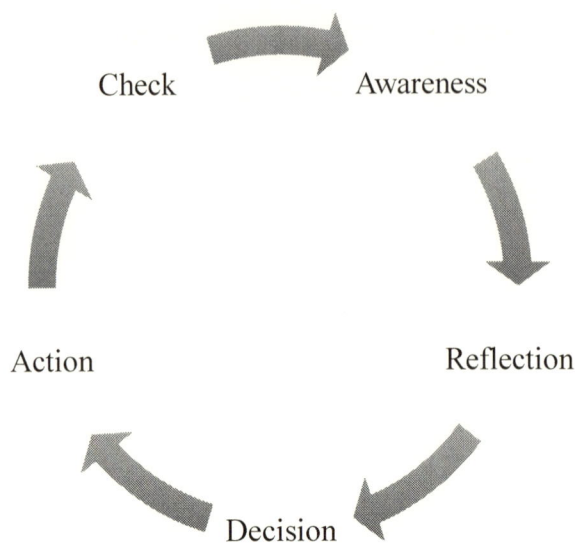

Awareness

According to Korn Ferry, one of the world's largest development organizations, the first step in any change sequence is awareness. In order for me to ever improve my performance, capitalize on my potential, or even make the best of my strengths, I must first be aware. Without awareness no person is ever motivated to act. The Price-Roberts model suggests that awareness is activated by means of self-assessment. Employees or associates are invited to assess themselves to determine their own strengths and gaps. The leader does not conduct the assessment. The Price-Roberts model further suggests that self-assessment reduces any fear or unhappiness associated with being evaluated by others. At the foundation of the Price-Roberts model is the imperative that the leader create a culture whereby each individual feels safe to be honest with himself or herself first. Also as part of the screening and/or onboarding process, asking job candidates to take a self-assessment is a prudent idea.

Reflection

The second step in the Price-Roberts model consists in having an internal focus. Each associate is invited to go inward and review what he or she has experienced as a result of his or her existing assignment or past experiences. The purpose of this reflection is not to incite guilt or shame, or to dwell in the rear-view mirror of one's journey. The purpose of this reflection process is to be authentically introspective and compare desired results with achieved outcomes. Each associate is then invited to review those areas where there was alignment between desired outcomes and achieved outcomes instead those times where misalignment occurred. The leader's only job during this portion of the process is to be supportive, nonjudgmental, and to help identify themes. The leader can be very instrumental in helping the employee or associate identify what tools and suggestions to enhance rapid growth apply to him or her personally.

Decision

The third step in the Price-Roberts model is the decision point. At this stage in the process each associate is invited to embrace a tool or to experiment with the practice that would help him or her achieve the larger goal, be true to himself or herself, embrace the concept of team, or satisfy the needs of the constituents, students, patients, or customers. While awareness is the first step in the Price-Roberts model, this decision point is where being motivated to act comes to life. This is where two-way communication and action-oriented feedback are critical. Until this point every action has been one of thought and not one of commitment. At this stage in the process the leader's role is to encourage deciding on and documenting actions that represent items to which the employee or associate can fully commit.

Action

The fourth step in the process is where the rubber meets the road. Many leaders get stuck here, but mostly because they want to start here. While action is critically important, it can be misguided without the first three steps in the process. In most instances, actions without analysis and data-gathering often lead to misalignment of pursuit. It is important to note that this step of the Price-Roberts model is where empathy and compassion might be tested. When employees or associates try out new skills, they may at times resort back to methods that have been unsuccessful in the past or contradictory to the stated mission and vision of the organization. That is why it is incredibly important to remember the seven second chances approach to leadership. This is where leaders will allow multiple opportunities for employees and associates to get it right. In this testing phase leaders are more likely to be successful if they prepare themselves for a few failures along the way. Although the empathetic and compassionate leadership approach contradicts and is the antithesis to the "sense of urgency" narrative of contemporary organizations, this approach has the potential to significantly impact and shift the organization's culture toward increased investment and commitment of its human resources.

Check

If not properly enforced, the "check" step in the process could be incorrectly perceived as evaluative. The purpose of the timely check-in is to make sure that the impacted associate or employee is achieving his or her own goals, aligning to his or her larger purpose, and supporting the organization. Again, the purpose is not punitive. Rather, the purpose is to gauge for alignment and to activate growth-oriented feedback. The check-in is not an evaluation; checking is a method to ensure that the leader does not falter on providing targeted support nor abandons shared accountability for action plans informed by the employee/associate and jointly decided upon. Within an empathetic culture, every employee should feel safe to confide in at least one person or team within the company; a sounding board can be especially helpful for employees experiencing empathy and compassion fatigue. During the "check" step of this model, organizations or teams must have the wherewithal to recognize when the empathetic and compassionate approach is necessary, and when the situation necessitates a different approach.

The Price-Roberts model must be rooted and grounded in the principles of the "seven second chances" approach, coupled and aligned with a relentless focus on being mission- and vision-focused as a team or organization. Essentially every team and organization should revisit or recreate, their mission, vision, and key strategies and align them to the organization or team member's daily actions. This alignment will enable leaders and their teams to calibrate their thoughts and actions around the following

- deciding on direction (informed by the organizational mission and vision)
- inspiring others (celebrating)
- driving outcomes (data-driven and focused on delivering on the mission)

These same leaders depend on a wide range of abilities, such as dealing with ambiguities, communicating vision and purpose, leveraging strengths, capitalizing on change, and maintaining effective working relationships (which includes conflict management). The way each individual approaches these topics is largely based on personality style. Anyone who has delivered a good number of 360-degree reviews may easily decipher a leader's personality type solely based on his or her highest and lowest competencies. This is because, even as you stretch yourself to learn new behaviors, your greatest assets will remain your greatest assets, and your weaknesses will rarely become strengths. For this reason, it is important to align leaders with the roles that best correspond to their strengths. This is the foundational work Marcus Buckingham shared in his book "Now Discover Your Strengths" and Jim Collins calls it "getting the right people on the bus."

What does this mean for empathetic and compassionate leadership? It means that we must understand what it's like to work daily in an area that aligns with our strengths. Conversely, we must understand what it's like to work daily in an area that aligns with our weaknesses. We know that people are more likely to be happy and effective, to give discretionary effort and commit to staying, if their jobs allow them to use their strengths regularly. If we are empathetic to this fact and understand this, our next step in the process is to be motivated to act on that knowledge, which means we need to assess the leadership styles of our people when we place them in leadership assignments. In the Price-Roberts model, the individual, not necessarily the leader, conducts the assessment. Therefore, the assessment would rarely, if ever, be used as a screening tool or as a primary criterion for job placement. However self-assessing leadership style could mean the difference between a leadership role that is fulfilling and rewarding versus one that is challenging and draining. Think of people who are unhappy in their jobs, (either because of the role or because of a misalignment between their passion and their assignment) you often see people who are not motivated, not maximizing their performance and therefore are not contributing to the team or organization in impactful ways. Conversely, individuals who are carefully matched in the correct roles inspire their team mates and other members of the organization to act. The empathic and compassionate leader is deliberate about matching the person with their purpose, passion, and their skills or prowess.

Purpose, Passion, Prowess

Purpose

In the reflection stage of the Price-Roberts model, ask leaders to reflect on what they love to do, where they like to do it, and with whom they like to do it. For many leaders, purpose is hard to identify at times because, when a person is aligned to their "purpose work," the work seems to be done effortlessly. Encourage leaders at all levels to consider what people always lean on them for, to identify what they make time for even when they're super-busy. They may not have considered that *that's* what they could be doing with their whole lives.

In the absence of this information, leaders do have the ability to create a shared purpose. This is where focusing on the mission and vision of the organization can be helpful. If the mission and vision are inspiring, if they incite excitement, then leaders can rally people behind the shared purpose versus the individual purpose. In these cases, the question is less about what the individual is designed to do and more about the greater need of the world at large and about how the organization, with the help of all the individuals who encompass it, may satisfy that need.

While empathy and compassion normally run out, a constant focus on the overarching purpose generates the energy necessary to keep moving forward in spite of whatever obstacles may arise.

Passion

Engagement is inevitable when passion is part of the work. Do you want a culture of engagement? Align leadership *passion* to the work. Ask your leaders, "What's the work you'd do for free?" Discretionary effort is one of the critical components of Gallup's definition of the term "engagement": How much effort do people give of their own desire?

Passion fuels the effort engine. Passion is what keeps you going when others would get tired and quit. Leaders have a unique challenge: they have to worry specifically about engagement, and they not only have to worry about the engagement of others, but they have to worry about engagement within themselves. Passion provides leaders with the sincerity to show up every day with the energy they need for their own work *and* enough left over to lead their teams.

One answer that leaders always give as a reason why they do not consistently practice empathetic and compassionate leadership is a "lack of time." When you are leading others, the meetings, and decisions, and performance reviews, and everything else, take time. The clock is further burdened with the reflection time, self-assessments, shared decision-making, and regular checkpoints. However, it is important to note that good outcomes are directly tied to a keen focus on people relationships. Leaders who focus on the shared purpose of an inspiring mission and vision can generate passion where it might otherwise be lacking.

Empathy and compassion in leadership is much about leading and inspiring in a way that you truly believe will positively impact the lives of others. It is morally repugnant and self-deprecating to be a part of a team, organization, or pursuit that you do not truly care about or have passion for. Caring, truly caring about your work is aligned to empathy.

The Power of Seven Second Chances

Have you ever worked in an organization or been a part of a team where people's discussion about caring and their actual actions were clearly misaligned? Armed with this knowledge, did you find yourself shaking your head in disapproval whenever they made pretentious public declarations whose eloquence masked their ugly and un-empathetic truth? The intentional pursuit of an empathetic and compassionate leadership journey should not supplant the other proven and impactful leadership competencies. However, there is the potential for incredible power and unprecedented impact when you combine empathetic and compassionate leadership with resilient leadership, instructional leadership, culturally-competent leadership, and even dictatorial leadership. In many professional arenas, there are the majority of people whose commitment to understanding the needs of those whom they serve and a willingness to take action to mitigate it, stops short if there is the likelihood that it will decrease their quality of life and own ambitious pursuits. Empathetic and compassionate leadership is not about allowing those who are affected to make excuses for apparent failure. It is *not* about fostering a culture that is soft on accountability, or one that stifles innovation and creativity. Empathetic and compassionate leadership is inclusive of a mission to cultivate the success of every stakeholder, regardless of title, and irrespective of the approach. But know that without passion or true care and concern, these efforts will fall short.

Prowess

Leadership skill is important. Professional development cannot be emphasized enough. Knowing the leader's purpose and passion is not sufficient if such knowledge doesn't overlap with skill or prowess. Absent a relentless focus on providing 10,000 hours of on-the-job experience for people to learn leadership skills, you will notice failures. In his book "You Already Know How to be Great," Alan Fine writes that people know what to do, yet sometimes they just lack the faith, the fire, or the focus. But people tend to miss another one of Fine's points, which is that knowledge is sometimes an issue. If people don't have knowledge, we have to work to fix that. One major gap in leadership skill or knowledge is that people often don't know what to discuss in coaching sessions. In fact, the word "coaching" has even started to take on a negative connotation. For this reason, the Price-

Roberts model uses the term "thought partnership" to refer to coaching.

Alan Fine, who is also the founder of InsideOut Development, has created one of the most comprehensive coaching approaches, a coaching model effective because of its simplicity. He breaks down which coaching conversations to have and when. However, Fine does something else that is critical. He delineates when coaching is necessary and when *advice-giving* is necessary instead. Sometimes there are knowledge gaps. This is especially true in

- new leadership situations
- transitions from being a technical professional to being a leader
- people working in a new leadership environment
- people new to middle or senior leadership
- roles where there is a right way (i.e. highly technical roles)

It is not always a knowledge issue, but sometimes it is. If you are trying to lead an empathetic and compassionate life,

Price-Roberts Model

what does this mean for you? Acknowledge that there is a leadership learning curve that needs to be addressed in each of the transitions. You cannot be empathetic to things you won't acknowledge. Acknowledge the hours it takes to develop mastery of something. Embrace the fact that you will not be able to identify a need today and eliminate that need tomorrow; such overnight success would require only 24 hours, yet an additional 9,976 hours would still need to transpire in order for an individual to become a master. We have to give leaders on-the-job training opportunities and close their skill gaps at every level of leadership. This is an essential step for building solid leadership in any company and it takes support and time.

Reflection Questions

1. What aspects of the Price-Roberts model resonate with you? When do you anticipate using the Price-Roberts model? What resistance do you expect to receive, if any? What strategies will you utilize to gain buy-in?

2. In an organization that is using the Price-Roberts model to create a culture of empathy and compassion, in what ways can the leadership team use the concept of the trickle-down effect to encourage time for reflection? Be specific.

3. What is necessary or required of a leadership team and/or organization to activate a system of authentic dialogue throughout the model? How can empathy and compassion be used to support development regardless of results during the "check" phase?

CHAPTER SEVEN OPTIMUM CONDITIONS FOR SUCCESS

Accountability

As stated earlier, any discussion about empathy and compassion will quickly evolve into a conversation about "accountability." Publicly leaders will buy-in but privately the question becomes this: How can an empathetic and compassionate approach *truly* result in positive outcomes? The lack of accountability can be easily described using the 1920 experiment conducted by C.H. Turner. If you are familiar with some of Nicole Price's previous work, you have likely heard about Turner's research, which consists of several steps to arrive at a fascinating conclusion. First you put fleas in a glass and watch them easily jump out of the glass. Then you put fleas in a glass and put a lid over that glass. The fleas will jump and hit their bodies against the lid until they realize it hurts. At that point they will start to jump just below the lid. Once all the fleas are jumping just below the lid, the lid may be removed, but the fleas will never jump out of the glass. This phenomenon is the reverse of accountability. Accountability suggests that you will take responsibility for your outcomes while if you have ever been like the fleas, you have likely experienced a situation where you have tried really hard at something and consistently experienced painful failure. Those failures have created a belief in your mind that there are obstacles or lids when they don't actually exist. Consequently, you lack the confidence to live as fully as you were designed to live. In the case of the fleas, they feel no responsibility (or even ability) to jump out of the glass. Although they are designed as incredible jumpers who'd always been capable of jumping out of the glass, they have learned to be helpless and they don't believe they can.

Leaders experience learned helplessness, too, just as all other humans on the planet. Most people have the capacity to express empathy and compassion. That does not change when they become leaders. When people don't express empathy and compassion as leaders they, too, have typically had a series of experiences that have limited their belief in its effectiveness. Belief is one of the critical components that fuels the rest of the empathetic and compassionate engine. Leaders must believe in the foundational idea that it can and will work.

Supporting Empathy and Compassion

There are several things that help create an empathetic and compassionate work environment that trickle down and impacts every person.

1. **Belief.** Perhaps people have failed you in the past. Perhaps your experiences during your professional pursuits were all anchored in situations where the culture was not permissive of tapping into the humanistic side of personnel. Perhaps *your* people are really tough cases. If you believe empathy and compassion will positively impact the environment, they will. If you believe that they won't, they will not. You should know that your mind is powerful, and that whatever you believe to be true will manifest itself. In 5 percent of the cases we encounter in our work, people exhaust all their chances and don't turn things around. That is a low number. The 95% success rate we see is caused by a litany of reasons, but a primary reason is that we have been relentless in our belief that that all people have a unique purpose or, to return to Turner's experiment, we believe all fleas can

jump out of the glass naturally. Sometimes the challenges we see are not skill-related issues. The question really is: do we *believe* people have the skill? In order for us to believe that others are capable of doing great work we also have to believe in our own innate ability to show up empathetically and compassionately.

2. **Lid Removal.** Sometimes, a person or system will place a "lid" or obstacle in our way. First, don't be one of these people. Do not accept the idea that only a select few individuals have what it takes to deliver. If you buy this concept you will suffocate others; you will reduce their power; you will leave them out. What are the "lids" we place on people that prevent them from stepping fully into their roles? What are the ways that we can break down those barriers to create space and freedom for people to lead in different ways, ways that better meet the needs of their specific work group or area? We have a responsibility to remove obstacles when we see them. This is especially important when we're in positions of power. Using the analogy of the fleas in the glass, there was a person who put the lid on the glass that caused the

helpless feelings. It is easy to tout accountability when you are outside the glass, but what are you doing to help those who are inside the glass? If we are going to do anything to impact the persistent leadership challenges that plague our organizations and hinder our culture efforts, we have to include a "lid removal plan" in the conversation.

3. **Be Open.** Open your mind to the possibility that old obstacles may no longer be challenges today. Perhaps you have written off some people. Open your mind. What are these people doing incredibly well? How can you build on those strengths? Sometimes imaginary lids are the hardest to break through, and that's because they work in our minds, where we generate our efforts and motivations. We are hardly a match for the power of our own minds. Just for today, imagine that no one you encounter has a skill gap or an issue that can't be overcome. What do you know about the person(s) under your supervision who are not meeting the team or organizational expectations as measured by the key performance indicators? What if the real problem were

simply a lack of self-confidence fueled by consistent encounters with negativity and disbelief? If that were the case, what could you do to rebuild confidence?

4. **Distinguish Sympathy from Empathy.** As simplistic as this may seem, distinguish sympathy from empathy (see introduction). The leaders' role includes understanding and navigating the organizational political environment and culture. Emotional empathy requires that those of us in positions of policy and influenced by those politics may find ourselves in a conundrum when faced with the choice of which among the dozens of appropriate leadership competencies to embrace. It is a normal response for individuals to confuse sympathy with empathy, thereby using the terms interchangeably. Leading from a place of sympathy, or feeling sorry for someone, can perpetuate mediocrity and encourage inaction. While sympathetic leadership approaches will not effectively address issues of disproportionality, a healthy balance of empathetic leadership with a shared system of accountability can result in a results oriented culture.

Optimum Conditions for Success

Let's imagine someone on the team has demonstrated mediocre performance and feels like s/he has a valid excuse. What do you do? We have a real example, Jane was serving as an assistant principal and wanted to interview for the principal role. Everyone on the team believed that based on Jane's experience she would perform exceptionally. During the interview, she performed poorly – totally bombed. Her answers were off target. She seemed unprepared and worse, she appeared unqualified. She returned the next day with an amazing excuse. In a follow-up conversation with her manager, she blamed her subpar performance on medication she was prescribed which had "confusion" listed as a side-effect. She believed that because she had a valid excuse, that her supervisor should sympathize with her. Jane thought that he should feel sorry for her. On the contrary, the leader was honest. He told Jane, "That was the worst interview performance I have ever seen. In fact, I don't believe I've ever seen worse. However, I am placing you in the role because I believe in your potential." Jane smiled and said, "Thank you." From experience with this leader, she now knows the expectation is high. She was not given an out. She screwed up. He was honest about that but he also let her know that he believes in her ability based on that last year's performance. This approach gets its fair share of criticism but we assert that leaders can be honest and kind. We also believe that you can understand a person's predicament and still invite her to perform at a higher level. This belief doesn't stop the criticism.

On December 2, 2016 the Wall Street Journal featured an article titled "The Perils of Empathy," written by Paul Bloom. Our practical and evidenced-based experience, coupled with the knowledge of the plethora of research that echoes the powerful impact of empathetic and compassionate leadership on organizational success inspired us to reflect and offer a different perspective that doesn't include the word "perils."

The Wall Street Journal article caused concern for us in the first paragraph. In the initial paragraph, the author appeared to cross the wires between empathy and sympathy. This confusion, and we alluded to it earlier, is understandable and is a common mistake in academia and other professional arenas. The article pointed out that trying to feel the pain of others (sympathy) in the professional environment is a bad idea. On the contrary, it should be noted that empathy is the understanding of another not the feeling of another's pain. The article's stance gives the impression that in order to survive in the arenas of policy and politics, one must be heartless as a leader. We couldn't disagree more. The lack of empathy is essentially an unwillingness to understand the pain, failure, and suffering of others and having a willingness to take action to alleviate that pain, failure, and suffering. Essentially the article, and those individuals whose beliefs are aligned to it, is often thought provoking but limited because of sweeping generalizations. Yes, the arena of K-12 education is riddled with aspects of policy and politics; however, built into every policy and political decision are children and people who are committed to alleviating the struggles and improving the trajectory of the lives of those children. After dissecting that article and the similarly aligned dogma of others, it is a sobering reminder that there is a lack of understanding the necessity of empathy in our everyday actions. As it relates to our work, we believe that there is an empathy deficit amongst the cadre of today's leaders. Since empathetic and compassionate leadership are competencies that can be shared and developed through capacity building efforts, there is tremendous hope for teams and organizations, as well as a nation-wide shift in our leadership requirements and practices to include empathetic leadership as a necessary competency. In response to the article's assertion and discouraging of the practice of empathy in policy and politics, we uplifted a reminder that policy and politics are not people businesses. They are often ivory-tower conceptualizations that rarely take into account the human element of impact. Conversely, teaching, leading, and serving in a high need, under supported, and underserved community is a people focused pursuit. Yes, the article referenced several examples that support its point, a few of which we agreed with. For example, he is correct in his assertion that leaders must be more objective in political arenas. This is true because a common set of beliefs is not always apparent across political lines. In these cases, objectivity is warranted. There was also an inference that leaders tend to practice perverse, moral mathematics; selectively choosing who they will and won't grant empathy and compassion based on favoritism. However, our thoughts on this particular point as it relates to our work in education and health service organizations, is that it would behoove them to implement a practices where they find ways to practice empathy and compassion regularly. It is so important that candidates who apply for leadership positions should be screened for empathy and compassion, and a culturally responsive leadership proclivity.

5. **Humility** is the ability and willingness to see yourself as an equal with everyone you lead and encounter. It is a modest view of oneself. Leaders who lack humility can become dictatorial and try to create change through force. Consequently, without humility leaders run the risk of losing the ability to inspire at the onset. Furthermore, it also makes it very difficult for them to be receptive to a variety of perspectives around critical

issues. To lead from a place of empathy and compassion, one *must* invoke a stance of humility. Leaders often struggle to acknowledge that the world does not revolve around them. Empathetic and compassionate leadership requires a leader to become self-actualized and unselfish in his or her leadership journey; it requires acknowledging that data is necessary, outcomes are important, but also people matter. Empathetic and compassionate leadership sometimes requires leaders to believe that every decision they make will have an impact on the lives of everyone with whom they come into contact. Empathetic and compassionate leadership inevitably results in the enhancement and increased longevity of the professional lives of those on the delivering and receiving end of this leadership display. Nelson Mandela's journey is a good example of empathy and humility in leadership. Mandela, the former president of South Africa, spent 27 years in prison after being charged with treason and given a life sentence. Mandela demonstrated empathy and humility as he genuinely engaged with the individuals and mechanisms that imprisoned him. He saw even his enemies as human beings whose beliefs and value systems differed from his own. Mandela made it clear to his closest aides that he had no intention of dehumanizing his opponents. Mandela continuously recognized humanity in all people even after he was president of South Africa. He could have used his role to belittle and punish his former oppressors. Instead he sought to understand them. He tried to find ways to bring people together. He always tried to understand his stakeholders and find helpful ways to help everyone save face and

6. **Selflessness** "If we think only of ourselves, forget about other people, then our minds occupy very small area. Inside that small area, even tiny problem appears very big. But the moment you develop a sense of concern for others, you realize that, just like ourselves, they also want happiness; they also want satisfaction. When you have this sense of concern, your mind automatically widens. At this point, your own problems, even big problems, will not be so significant. The result? Big increase in peace of mind. One of the stories of this century that echoes this point occurred in Nanjing, China. The Nanjing Yangtze

River Bridge was known as one of the most perilous suicide spots in the world. Once a week, someone jumps to his or her death. Annually, 200,000 teenage girls, couples jumping hand in hand, and hordes of men and women account for the "bodies raining to their end" from the bridge. This brings us to Mr. Chen Si, a resident of Nanjing who works as a functionary for a transportation company. Shortly after reading an article about the suicides, he began to spend his entire days at the south tower of the bridge waiting for opportunities to pull or talk would-be jumpers from death. Chen Si was not expecting anything in return for his time spent observing possible suicide takers. He didn't consider the sacrifice but because of his selflessness, a small number of the people who Chen Si saved started an annual ritual to gather and celebrate their new lives; a life since being saved on the bridge – lives the world needs.

7. **Identify the Non-Negotiables.** Every successful leader knows that there is a set of team and organizational non-negotiables even when leading with empathy and compassion. But keep in mind that even when the non-

negotiables are violated, the first step after the coaching, courageous conversation or evaluation should not be criticism but rather an attempt to understand, accompanied by the motivation to help. However, there are situations where no matter what a leader wants to do his or her hands are tied. Contrary to popular belief, this is not a long list. Here are some examples in some specific industries

- In most industries – being found guilty of sexual harassment or assault
- Education – child abuse
- Banking – theft
- Healthcare – confidentiality breaches
- Retail – discrimination

This list is not comprehensive or exhaustive but we believe that theft alone does not warrant criticism, exclusion and/ or termination. In most jobs, we challenge leaders to avoid looking at the presenting problem and consider that there may be something else to evaluate. Immediate termination is easy. What does it look like to decide that we are going to use empathy and compassion in these situations? Do you think that a person who gets caught stealing is just as likely to steal again from the same employer if given another chance? Maybe you can't get your mind around stealing. What about lying? Insubordination? Making quality errors?

Listen, in this duo at times even we are split. Dr. Roberts has been leading this way for a very long time. Nicole has to work hard at the empathetic and compassionate approach when leaders under her tutelage seem undeserving. This approach will require courage because often you will find many people to agree with a harsh approach when lying, cheating, stealing and harming are involved. However, managerial courage is foundational to leadership roles. It is your job when you are a leader. Unfortunately, when you mention "managerial courage" people think about having the harsh conversations. We invite you to think of it differently. Taking an approach that is unconventional is courageous but it is not as difficult as we envision if we take time as leaders to consider our values. What do you as a leader value? According to Korn Ferry Leadership Architect the reason people have lower skill in practicing managerial courage is because they fear being wrong, fear losing, fear getting emotional or fear being out in front. In fact, almost all of the cited reasons revolve around fear.

True courage is understanding that it is natural to feel fear as an emotion. It is also important to know that when we are afraid we often exaggerate the possible outcomes. We misjudge the probable dangers and underestimate the potential rewards of stepping forward and doing it scared. We think, "What if I give this person another chance and they screw up again? What will be the reflection on me?"

This is relevant when we talk about empathy and compassion in leadership. It is paradoxical to combine courage with a topic like empathy and compassion however in our experiences, being empathetic and compassionate on a regularly basis requires all the courage you can muster when someone has done something "wrong" more than once or when their offense something we would have normally addressed without empathy and compassion. People support empathy and compassion when they feel the subject is deserving. In our lives at work that translates to those times when things are going well or when we are dealing with people who have, what we perceive to be, small performance gaps.

Sure. Be empathetic and compassionate when it doesn't take courage to do so but what about when our associates have huge gaps in performance? What about when our trust has been violated? What about when, for whatever reason, I don't think you deserve empathy or compassion? That's precisely when courage matters.

All we are asking is that you try empathy and compassion out as your first option. If you struggle to do it with your hardest cases, start with the easier ones first. We have far too many examples of leaders not practicing empathy and compassion with even their "best" employees. We believe we can change the world and you can practice with this group if you feel unsafe or unsure.

What if we busted up the evaluation-to-termination cycle and interrupted the process at evaluation? What if when we noticed there was an issue we stopped and said how can I

Optimum Conditions for Success

better understand (empathy) and then be motivated to actually help (compassion)?

In fact, every time you notice yourself evaluating and the results are negative, I want you to ask

- Have I had an experience like this before? Have I done something similar?
- How might a reasonable person end up in this situation?
- What can I do to help make this situation better?

What's the worst that can happen if you refuse to go to criticism? On the flip side what is at stake to gain if you dig in, take a risk on *those* people and decide to provide support and help? Our current times are calling for courageous leaders who will stand up and stand out for attempting to understand the basic human condition of falling short sometimes. With that, the list of non-negotiables is not printed in a 100-page handbook – the list is short.

Conclusion

The role of the leader on every team and within every organization is to achieve the mission and established bottom line. The approach that every leader utilizes to achieve the aforementioned varies from person to person, by organization, and certainly by geographic location. The research about leadership style and the competencies that ensure success can be found in many books, as well as the educational programs of the most prestigious schools around the world. Although there is a plethora of data and guidance about leadership styles and their effectiveness in many industries, there is a paucity of data and investment when it comes to the utilization of empathy and compassion as a leadership approach. This is primarily because of the unpopular nature of this highly effective and under-utilized leadership philosophy and approach. Now that you are at the conclusion of this work, we are certain that your confidence to pivot towards or at least to infuse the empathetic and compassionate leadership approach has increased. The Price-Roberts Model is meant to serve as a resource in which one can anchor their approach in both their professional and

Optimum Conditions for Success

personal pursuit. We are not vehemently opposed to the traditional or frequently utilized leadership philosophies and approaches; however, we make the argument that an empathetic and compassionate leadership approach can be a value add for individuals, small teams, or large organizations. An empathetic and compassionate approach transcends the professional arena and can be beneficial in personal relationships and marriages.

In organizations that include the military, health care, education, and athletics, there needs to be a radical reorganization and reset of the approach to leadership. In the context of the contemporary political landscape, it would behoove us to embrace, engage with, and encourage empathy and compassion. Adding the element of humanity and dignity to our daily interactions with everyone will significantly change the way that we do business. A society that anchors its core values in empathy and compassion in word and deed will take the following stance:

- Reduce instead of increase its prison incarceration rates.

- Be intentional about closing the proverbial achievement and opportunity gap.
- Encourage the equitable treatment of every person regardless of gender, sexual orientation, race, or ethnicity.
- Increase organizations willingness to place people and personnel before outcomes and the bottom-line
- Will see and discourage the criminalization of minorities, but instead, engage with them on the merits of their abilities.
- Erode the incendiary rhetoric that perpetuates anger, tension, and ultimately violence amongst groups, classes, and races that will be destructive to all

The necessity to lead lives that celebrates an empathetic and compassionate approach to our existence is the missing ingredient to the pursuit of happiness at work and at home.

Optimum Conditions for Success

Reflection Questions - Will empathy and compassion work when... (Hint: try asking, "will understanding and being motivated to help work...")

1. What if an employee appears to have exhausted every coaching and professional development offering?
2. What if someone is known to exhibit a defeatist mentality and conduct that causes a disruption for the bottom-line?
3. What if someone clearly states and demonstrates that they will not be invested in the organization's core values?
4. What if an employee exhibits discriminatory and prejudiced displays towards colleagues or other stakeholders?
5. What if an employee is proven to be a stranger of the truth, and continuously gives "alternative to the facts?"
6. What if someone misrepresents the organization?
7. What if someone demonstrates that they cannot be entrusted with confidential and sensitive information?

8. What if a leader does not "walk the talk?" What strategies can be employed?
9. What if the leader believes empathy and compassion is innate versus something that can be learned or taught? What do you believe?

About the Authors
Biographical Information

Nicole D. Price believes two things: 1) If leadership is anything, it's personal 2) Everyone can be a great leader. Her session participants give glowing reviews and often request repeat appearances. She'll make you laugh; she'll make you think; she'll make you better. Nicole is the owner of the leadership development company, Lively Paradox where they specialize in combining accountability with empathy and compassion as a fundamental leadership strategy. Nicole received her B.S. in chemical engineering from North Carolina A&T University and her master's degree in adult education from Park University.

PUBLISHED WORKS
- Lively Paradox: An Authentic Perspective on Issues of Diversity & Inclusion
- Cultivating Culture

About the Authors

Dr. Ian A. Roberts is a school turnaround specialist whose work history includes being a Commissioned Army Officer; Law Enforcement Officer, Middle and High School Teacher and Principal for New York Board of Education, Baltimore City Schools, and District of Columbia Public Schools; Senior Vice-President for Lighthouse Academies Charter Schools, and Middle and High School Superintendent for St. Louis Public Schools. He has also served as an adjunct professor/lecturer in graduate schools and leadership programs and is a former Olympic Track and Field Athlete (2000 Olympic Games in Sydney, Australia).

- Post-Doctoral Studies/Institutes, **Harvard University Graduate School of Education**
- Doctorate in Urban Education Leadership, **Morgan State University**, Baltimore, MD
- Executive Master of Science, Executive Leadership, **Georgetown University**, Washington, DC
- Master of Science in Secondary Education, **St. John's University**, New York
- Bachelor of Science in Criminal Justice, **Coppin State University**, Baltimore, MD

PUBLISHED WORK

Prisoners or Presidents: The Simple Things that Change Everything; When Principals Lead Like Lives Depend on It

Bibliography

ADA – The American with Disabilities Act

Bloom, Paul – Against Empathy: The Case for Rational Compassion

Buckingham, Marcus – Now Discover Your Strengths

Collins, Jim – Good to Great

Compassion Fatigue Awareness Project

Dalai Lama

Einstein, Albert

Fine, Alan – You Already Know How to be Great

Goldman, Daniel – Social Intelligence – The New Science of Social Relationships

Holy Bible – King James Version

Bibliography

Hsieh, Tony - Happiness Matters: How to Create a Culture for Business to Thrive

IDEA (PL94-142) The Individuals with Disabilities Education Act

Korn Ferry International – FYI: For Your Improvement Competency Development Guide

Korn Ferry International – Interview Architect

Lochner, Lance – The Effect of Education on Crime: Evidence from Prison Inmates, Arrest, and Self-Reports

Mandela, Nelson

McGlore Elementary in Denver Colorado tagline: Happy children learn more

Monroe, Miles – Pursuit of Purpose

National Commission on Teaching for Americas Future (NCTAF)

O'Cadiz, Maria - Writer Education Week

Bibliography

Pew Partnership

Price, Nicole - Lively Paradox: An Authentic Perspective on Issues of Diversity and Inclusion

Roberts, Ian – Prisoners of Presidents: The Simple Things That Changes Everything When Principals Lead Like Lives Depend on it.

Si, Chen – On a Bridge of Sighs, the Suicidal Meet a Staying Hand

Turner, C.H. – Literature for 1910 on the Behavior of Spiders and Insects Other Than Ants

Empathy and Compassion Assessment

Rating Scale:

Mastery Effectively Empathetic	Proficient Empathetic	Progressing Somewhat Empathetic	Need Lacking Empathy
4	3	2	1

Personal Leadership

I evaluate my own practices in order to gauge efficiency and effectiveness.

    4   3   2   1

I believe I have the ability to grow.

    4   3   2   1

I set the tone for all stakeholders, adult relationships and practices in the organization.

    4   3   2   1

My style strikes a balance between being very firm about non-negotiables and being flexible about the how the work gets accomplished in order to leverage peoples' strengths.

    4   3   2   1

I am clear about my expectations so that all stakeholders can do their best work.

    4   3   2   1

I delegate as a means to develop my people.

    4   3   2   1

I relentlessly provide support and follow up to ensure targets are being met.

    4   3   2   1

I demonstrate genuine engagement with others, humility, and relationship-building.

    4   3   2   1

Empathy and Compassion Assessment

I own the team's failures and growth opportunities.

 4   3   2   1

I am committed to recognize that people truly matter; my daily actions and leadership stances are a clear indicator that I believe this.

 4   3   2   1

Resilient Leadership

I am willing to exhaust efforts at building capacity.

 4   3   2   1

I work to correct performance deficits in peers and colleagues.

 4   3   2   1

I am aware of the impact my leadership style has on my people.

 4   3   2   1

I consistently work to learn and understand the needs of my people.

 4   3   2   1

I make multiple attempts to use the strengths of my people to achieve operational excellence.

 4   3   2   1

I prioritize development.

 4   3   2   1

I create, implement, and institutionalize sustainable systems and processes that support professional development.

 4   3   2   1

Empathy and Compassion Assessment

Culturally Competent Leadership

I examine my own biases.
      4   3   2   1

I revisit my own dispositions, and biases with the goal of becoming more efficient and effective for daily operational excellence.
      4   3   2   1

I continuously dismantle inequitable and exclusionary practices.
      4   3   2   1

I create a fully inclusive environment where all stakeholders, regardless of ethnicity, race, ability level, or other social constructs, thrive and learn at high levels.
      4   3   2   1

I am aware of my own cultural worldview and attitude towards cultural differences.
      4   3   2   1

I am knowledgeable of different cultural practices and worldviews; and cross-cultural skills.
      4   3   2   1

I possess a high level of cultural competency and lead effectively across cultures.
      4   3   2   1

I create equitable practices recognizing that inequity is pervasive in the arena of education
      4   3   2   1

I am committed through daily actions to diligently provide opportunities for equity and quality in the workplace.
      4   3   2   1

Empathy and Compassion Assessment

Interpersonal Leadership

I build trusting relationships.

    4   3   2   1

I celebrate/credit my subordinates for team/organization success and goal achievement.

    4   3   2   1

I am committed to publicly praise.

    4   3   2   1

I am committed to privately correct colleagues for ineffective practice/underperformance.

    4   3   2   1

I facilitate active stakeholder communities dedicated to achieving the organizations mission.

    4   3   2   1

I have a relentless belief that everyone has the ability to continuously grow.

    4   3   2   1

I can see beyond deficits and recognize possible contributions regardless of an individual's academic, behavioral, or social deficits.

    4   3   2   1

I am successful at developing, building and supporting healthy teams.

    4   3   2   1

I believe that everyone should be invested in to execute the mission and vision of the organization.

    4   3   2   1

I practice shared accountability by not letting under performers off the hook.

    4   3   2   1

Empathy and Compassion Assessment

I intentionally discourage high performers/achievers from becoming professionally aloof.

       4   3   2   1

I am committed to the empowerment, encouragement, and uplifting of colleagues in an effortless manner.

       4   3   2   1

I am committed to correct, or if necessary chastise, violators of company policy (non-negotiables) in a manner that will not strip away dignity.

       4   3   2   1

Total = [ ]

Score Chart:

140+
Strong balance of empathetic & compassionate leadership

105 – 139
Inclination to lead with empathy and compassion

70 – 104
Clear empathetic and compassionate **developmental areas**

69 or below
Leader with compassion **deficits**

Made in the USA
Coppell, TX
09 May 2021